TOLKIEN'S WORLD

Tolkien's World

RANDEL HELMS

Boston

HOUGHTON MIFFLIN COMPANY

The author is grateful to George Allen and Unwin, Ltd.,
and Houghton Mifflin Company for permission to quote
from the published works of J. R. R. Tolkien.

Library of Congress Cataloging in Publication Data

Helms, Randel.
    Tolkien's world.

    Includes bibliographical references.
    1. Tolkien, John Ronald Reuel, 1892–1973 —
Criticism and interpretation.   I. Title.
PR6039.032Z66   828'.9'1209   74-1240
ISBN 0-395-18490-8

Printed in the United States of America

V   9   8   7   6   5   4   3

To Pennie and Kate,
for their love and presence

ACKNOWLEDGMENTS

I WISH to thank my friends and colleagues Drs. C. L. Batten, Jr., Joanna Dales, and Garth Dales for reading this work at various stages. They, and two fine editors at Houghton Mifflin, Mrs. Anne N. Barrett and Mr. Jeffrey Smith, kept my grosser errors from slouching into print. I am grateful also to the editors of *Literature and Psychology* and *Mythcon I Proceedings,* 1971 (The Mythopoeic Society, P. O. Box 4671, Whittier, CA 90607) for permission to reprint essays that originally appeared in their journals. Mr. Dennis Horn performed admirable labors on the manuscript and index. My greatest debt is acknowledged in the dedication.

TOLKIEN'S WORLD

An Introduction

THIS BOOK is for those who have come to love Tolkien's world and want to know more about it and how it came into being. "Love" is not too strong a word, for with *The Hobbit* and *The Lord of the Rings*, J. R. R. Tolkien has created an imaginary world so compelling, so real, that hundreds of thousands of people have read them not just once but several times. Why are they so appealing, even necessary, to so many people? What is there about them that goes deeper than mere adventure narrative? What are their roots?

Though the attempt to find a full answer to these questions in Tolkien's "sources" is not satisfactory, we may find the beginning of one in his reaction as critic to some of his sources. For as a professional scholar of Medieval British and European literature, Tolkien was a knowledgeable explorer of a number of imaginary worlds — the *middangeard* ("Middle-earth") of *Beowulf*, the grim and brutal cosmos of *The Völsunga Saga*, the cold and bitter realm of the *Eddas* — and all of them worked their sway over his own imagination, lodging there to ferment and bubble over into a new world, the Middle-earth of the hobbits. Tolkien's world is indeed traditional; borrowing from the power and import of his sources, recasting where necessary, he has out of the matrix of a dead and often misunderstood literature created an imaginary kingdom that though new is not groundless.

To call the ancient works "misunderstood" is to begin to grasp what Tolkien was trying to do, for this is to speak from his own point of view. When he had discovered, in writing *The Hobbit*, the possibilities of his own world of Middle-earth, he rediscovered, as a result, the value and relevance for our own time of mythic literature (his own not less than *Beowulf*). He found next that he had to convince an audience of this same value, for Tolkien's contemporaries had, in his view, lost the keys to mythic response. So he set about the task of schooling an entire generation to a renewed perception of an ancient value and truth. Tolkien once told a friend that he was distressed that the English had so few myths of their own and had to live on foreign borrowings, "so I thought I'd make one myself." *

It is the aim of this book to show how he has done this. We shall look, for the most part, not at Middle-earth's geographical analogues or literary sources but at its origins and meanings as a product of the creative imagination. What sort of imagination *does* Tolkien have? What are its strengths and limitations? In what forms does it exhibit itself, in what kinds of literature is it most free to pursue its own recognized or secret purposes? And what is there about *his* imagination that is so freeing and enriching to our own? I try to answer these questions with a study of the development of Tolkien's imaginative conception of Middle-earth, his own version of what he calls *Faërie*, an independent realm of the imagination with its own laws and significances, and with, as well, a strange relevance to our own world.

* Bill Cater, "More and More People Are Getting the J. R. R. Tolkien Habit," Los Angeles *Times* "Calendar," Sunday, April 9, 1972, p. 14.

Tolkien's world did not spring full-grown from his head like Minerva, nor did he fully grasp its implications and possibilities immediately on inventing it. Only slowly as he worked and reworked *The Hobbit* in the 1930s, and as he rethought the contemporary meanings and values of mythological literature in his essays on *Beowulf* and "On Fairy-Stories," did Tolkien grasp that what he had almost inadvertently discovered with Bilbo and his ring was a means not only of delighting vast numbers of people but equally a means of exploring and suggesting answers to some of the most profound questions and problems of the mid-twentieth century. Tolkien was much too modest to make such a claim for himself, so his critic must make it for him; and I shall make one more: *The Lord of the Rings* is one of the most wonderful and significant tales published in English since the Second World War. This book tells why I think so.

RANDEL HELMS

CONTENTS

Tolkien's World: An Introduction   ix

I. "I DESIRED DRAGONS"
The Development of a Theory of Fantasy   1

II. TOLKIEN'S LEAF
The Hobbit and the Discovery of a World   19

III. THE HOBBIT AS SWAIN
A World of Myth   41

IV. FRODO ANTI-FAUST
The Lord of the Rings as Contemporary Mythology   56

V. TOLKIEN'S WORLD
The Structure and Aesthetic of The Lord of the Rings   76

VI. THE MYTH ALLEGORIZED
Tolkien's Minor Prose   109

VII. LAST GLEANINGS FROM THE RED BOOK
Scholarly Parody in The Adventures of Tom Bombadil   126

AFTERWORD   148

Notes   155

Index   161

TOLKIEN'S WORLD

"I DESIRED DRAGONS"

The Development of
a Theory of Fantasy

> The dragon had the trade-mark *Of Faërie* written plain upon
> him. In whatever world he had his being it was an
> Other-world. Fantasy, the making or glimpsing of Other-
> worlds, was the heart of the desire of Faërie. I desired
> dragons with a profound desire.
>
> — TOLKIEN, "On Fairy-Stories"

AT LITERATURE's pivotal moments, a gifted writer redis-
covers a decayed or discredited literary form and then
creates an audience for it. One of these moments happened
about 1933, when J. R. R. Tolkien began telling his children
about a funny little creature named Bilbo, who found a magic
ring and invisibly stole a dragon's treasure. The stories grew
and were published in 1937 as *The Hobbit*. But this was only
the beginning; the implications of what he had made would
give Tolkien no rest, and the imaginative growth caused in
him by his children's book set up a creative turbulence lasting
through twenty years of nighttime off-duty writing, culminating at last in his fantasy masterpiece, *The Lord of the Rings*.
The hobbit stories conquered and remade Tolkien's imagination, reshaping even his responses to the literature he
studied as Rawlinson Professor of Anglo-Saxon at Oxford,
making him see with new eyes, so that he found himself,

under this profound new imaginative influence, rethinking the force and function of the mythological imagination, re-examining the meaning and validity of fantasy narrative. Throughout the later 1930s, Tolkien's critical and professional work related in a fascinating way to his creative work, closely paralleling and underpinning the development of his deepening imagination as he sought to understand critically where it was leading him. In his 1936 Israel Gollancz Memorial Lecture, *"Beowulf:* The Monsters and the Critics," and his 1938 Andrew Lang Lecture, "On Fairy-Stories," Tolkien came gradually to terms with the form that had captured him, described and evaluated it, slowly, carefully preparing himself and an audience for the book *The Hobbit* taught him how to write, the book he had already begun when he delivered the *Beowulf* lecture, *The Lord of the Rings.*

We cannot fully grasp the intent behind Tolkien's famous lecture on *Beowulf* before the British Academy in November 1936 unless we see that it is in part the beginning of his preparation of an audience for *The Hobbit,* published a few months later, and *The Lord of the Rings,* already in progress. Tolkien's imaginative response to the mythological narrative in *Beowulf* is in fact an eddy in the tremendous imaginative current that had already for many months been flowing into his own narrative of Middle-earth. In the lecture we see him, perhaps almost without realizing it, identify himself with the *Beowulf* poet and in his own defense, as it were, provide telling critical justifications for ancient poetic strategies he was even then reviving in his own work. His contemporaries, Tolkien argued, had forgotten that the mythological imagination could deal in a profoundly revelatory way with serious moral and spiritual issues. He himself had learned, through the creation of his mythological realm of Middle-earth, something very new and yet very old — that a living mythology can deepen rather than cloud our vision of reality; this is the truth he tries to communicate in the *Beowulf* lecture.

Previous critics of *Beowulf* had objected to its puerile conception of monsters; the poem's great flaw, W. P. Ker argued, lay in its presenting little besides the deaths of worms and ogres:

> The fault of *Beowulf* is that there is nothing much in the story. The hero is occupied in killing monsters . . . Beowulf has nothing else to do, when he has killed Grendel and Grendel's mother in Denmark: he goes home to his own Gautland, until at last the rolling years bring the Fire-drake and his last adventure. It is too simple . . . Yet with this radical defect, a disproportion that puts the irrelevances at the centre and the serious things on the outer edges, the poem of *Beowulf* is undeniably weighty.[1]

Tolkien's answering strategy is simply to reverse Ker's objection; the serious things in *Beowulf* are exactly at the center, and the most serious of all is the dragon himself: "the monsters are not an inexplicable blunder of taste; they are essential, fundamentally allied to the underlying ideas of the poem, which give it its lofty tone and high seriousness" (p. 68). Here is a distinctly striking moment in the history of the modern imagination, the resurgence of a critical grasp of the mythological perception of radical evil. Tolkien has taken the very stumbling block in the way of full imaginative response to *Beowulf*, turned it over, and discovered the poem's richest dark jewel, the dragon, that old serpent himself. In the face of an age long accustomed to reading heroic narrative through eyes focused by the lens of realistic fiction, and long accustomed to divorcing mythology from serious intellectual consideration, Tolkien defended dragons — defended in fact the urges of his own creative imagination.

Far from cheapening *Beowulf*, Tolkien argues, the monsters ennoble it with a vision of embodied radical evil, foe of God and man, against which no hero, however great, has hope of victory. "It is the strength of the northern mythological imagination that it faced this problem [of radical evil], put the monsters in the centre, gave them victory but no honour, and found a potent but terrible solution in naked will and courage." Tolkien's aim was to deny that this mode of "imagination has faded for ever into literary ornament" and to reassert that it has "power, as it were, to revive its spirit even in our own times" (p. 77). And it was, of course, reviving in his own works; Tolkien could hardly fail to think of his *Hobbit* and work-in-progress as he uttered his manifesto for dragons:

> A dragon is no idle fancy. Whatever may be his origins, in fact or invention, the dragon in legend is a potent creation of men's imagination, richer in significance than his barrow is in gold. Even to-day (despite the critics) you may find men not ignorant of tragic legend and history, who have heard of heroes and indeed seen them, who yet have been caught by the fascination of the worm. More than one poem in recent years . . . has been inspired by the dragon of *Beowulf* (pp. 64–65).

The mythological imagination, Tolkien argues, is still necessary for a full understanding of *Beowulf*; and it is here, in the mythological perception of radical evil, that he finds the worth of dragons, both for the British Academy and for himself. There are no heroes (and we do need them) unless there be dragons as well: "as far as we know anything about these old poets, we know this: the prince of the heroes of the North, supremely memorable . . . was a dragon slayer . . . Fáfnisbani." Wherever there is heroic narrative in Norse and ancient English, there are "these two primary features: the dragon, and the slaying of him as the chief deed of the greatest of heroes" (p. 64).

Tolkien has, of course, hit upon a truth about the human imagination here — that, when richly at work, it will "mythicize" any memorable human action. Mircea Eliade tells the case of the historical Dieudonne de Gozon, third Grand Master of the Knights of St. John at Rhodes, who slew in legend the dragon of Malpasso. It matters not, says Eliade, that the historical documents of the time make no mention of dragons; the mere fact that de Gozon was in the popular imagination a hero necessarily identified him "with a category, an archetype, which, entirely disregarding his real exploits, equipped him with a mythical biography from which it was *impossible* to omit combat with a reptilian monster." [2]

Tolkien will argue elsewhere that the mythological imagination is necessary to a vital religion; he attempts to persuade us in the *Beowulf* lecture that it is equally requisite for an imaginatively vital response to heroic literature. His method is to counter a standard criticism of *Beowulf* in his time — that the Anglo-Saxons "could not . . . keep Scandinavian bogies and the Scriptures separate in their puzzled brains" (p. 68), that the poem is, in other words, a confused and deeply flawed mixture of pagan and Christian. Tolkien urges that this very fusion is the source of much of the poem's power. The *Beowulf* poet, standing as he did in a moment of cultural shift, pagan to Christian, already himself on the Christian side but still imaginatively alive to the ancient traditions, was able to view his tales from a very special perspective: *"at once they became more ancient and remote, and in a sense darker"* (p. 71). "He could view from without, but still feel immediately and from within, the old dogma." We have, therefore, in *Beowulf,* "a poem from a pregnant moment of poise, looking back into the pit, by a man learned in old tales who was struggling, as it were, to get a general view of them all, perceiving their common tragedy of inevitable ruin, and yet feeling this more *poetically* because he was himself removed from the direct pressure of its despair" (p. 73). Tolkien's insight into *Beowulf's* power has by now become a commonplace about the poem, but what must strike us like a blow if we read more closely here is that this is not only a powerful defense of the mythological vision in *Beowulf,* it is an equally powerful defense of Tolkien's own vision of Middle-earth. For his position *vis-à-vis* the world of *The Hobbit* and *The Lord of the Rings* is precisely that of the *Beowulf* poet toward the world of the Fire-drake. Both visions are works of a "learned man writing of old times" the charm of which has much to do with their being "heathen, noble and hopeless" (p. 78). Both are works deeply tinged with Christianity, but in which the "specifically Christian was suppressed" (p. 72). Finally, both are works the power of which comes from a fusion of the "creed of unyielding will" (p. 70) on the one hand, with a momentously adjusted perception of pagan mythological monsters on the other. That adjustment involves the two writers' Christianity, for from a Christian perspective, the monsters of both *Beowulf* and *The Lord of the Rings* are not only "the enemies of mankind," but also "inevitably the enemies of the one God, *ece Dryhten*" (p. 72), not just pagan bogies, but "images of the evil spirit" himself (p. 73). Tolkien, "inspired by the dragon of Beowulf" like the poets he mentions, has created his own "image of the evil spirit," Sauron, Lord of the Rings, and his attempt to deepen his contemporaries' imaginative response to ancient visions of that evil has obviously found its source as much in the artist's need of an audience as it has in scholarly interests. For imaginative response to Grendel and the dragon is a prime means of learning to respond to the mythic perceptions of *The Lord of the Rings*.

I doubt, however, that Tolkien fully succeeded in convincing his audience, sober British scholars all, of the human value of myth; indeed he scarcely tried, averring a disinclination to "attempt at length a defence of the mythical mode of imagination, and the disentanglement of the confusion between myth and folk-tale" he felt was rife in his time. He went no farther, in this lecture, than the fairly cryptic remark that myth is man's one imaginative act "capable in poetic hands . . . of becoming largely significant — as a whole, accepted unanalyzed" (p. 63). The reason, I suppose, is that he felt no need, in 1936, to do more than justify the role of monsters in an imaginative response to *Beowulf*; the time was yet to come when he would be forced to work out the implications of the larger question in which monsters form but a part — the nature and value of mythology itself.

Tolkien's defense of the mythical mode of the imagination had to wait until he had reached a point, well into the writing of *The Lord of the Rings*, from which he was constrained to pull back and take stock. That moment came in 1938, when he found that the leaf first called *The Hobbit* was growing into a mighty tree. Tolkien's attempts to understand what was happening in his imagination in 1938, to work out for

himself the meaning of the frightening and foreboding transformation of Bilbo's magic toy into Frodo's One Ring of
Power, resulted in the writing of the lecture "On Fairy-
Stories." In his Introductory Note to the 1964 reissue of this
work under the title *Tree and Leaf*, Tolkien explains that it
was "written in the same period (1938–39), when *The Lord
of the Rings* was beginning to unroll itself and to unfold
prospects of labour and exploration in yet unknown country
as daunting to me as to the hobbits. At about that time
we had reached Bree, and I had then no more notion than
they had of what had become of Gandalf or who Strider
was; and I had begun to despair of surviving to find out."[3]
Tolkien had, in other words, hit a dry spell, suffered a
momentary imaginative inhibition, chiefly because he was
not sure what ground he stood on with his new work,
altogether different in tone from *The Hobbit*. He was in
"unknown country," and in order once again to find his
coordinates, he had to shift briefly from map-making to
map-reading, from creation to critical manifesto. To find
out who Strider was, and whither Gandalf had gone, Tolkien
had to restudy the realm wherein they lived, the perilous
realm of Faërie.

So he took advantage of an invitation to deliver the 1938
Andrew Lang Lecture at the University of Saint Andrews
to consider once again the vexing question he had tactfully
avoided in 1936: what is the power of mythology? In 1936
Tolkien had gone no farther than to put his finger on the
weakness of the usual answers to that question, observing
that "It is possible, I think, to be moved by the power of
myth and yet to misunderstand the sensation, to ascribe it
wholly to something else that is also present: to metrical
art, style, and verbal skill" (p. 64). Two years later, he was

forced by his developing imagination into the next level of definition.

Caught in his dry spell of 1938, Tolkien no longer felt disinclined to pursue the question of the role of the mythological imagination. This time he began by tackling head-on the vulgar error that myths are simply crudely "scientific" allegorical explanations of natural phenomena, that, for example, the "Olympians were *personifications* of the sun, of dawn, of night, and so on, and [that] all the stories told about them were originally *myths* (*allegories* would have been a better word) of the greater elemental changes and processes of nature" (TL, p. 23). Mythology is a much profounder activity of the human imagination; indeed Tolkien half-humorously suggests that Max Müller's dictum "mythology is a disease of the language" ought to be reversed: "It would be more near the truth to say that languages, especially modern European languages, are a disease of mythology" (TL, p. 21). Speaking more strictly, he posits that the "incarnate mind, the tongue, and the tale are in our world coeval"; for the aboriginal perceptive act, seeing green grass and grasping that "it is *green* as well as being *grass*," was also the aboriginal imaginative act: the "mind that thought of *light, heavy, grey, yellow, still, swift,* also conceived of magic that would make heavy things light and able to fly, turn grey lead into yellow gold, and the still rock into a swift water . . ., and put hot fire into the belly of the cold worm. But in such 'fantasy,' as it is called, a new form is made; *Faërie* begins; Man becomes a sub-creator" (TL, pp. 21–22). It is clear that the Lang Lecture involves a continuation of the same thinking about mythology and its functions that informs the Gollancz Lecture. But in 1938 Tolkien enriches or at least complicates the discussion with some new terms; we shall see, however, that the "new" terms are merely a way of reinvigorating an ancient but currently discredited critical tradition.

Even though the Lang Lecture continues a concern with mythology, Tolkien prefers to shift his terms, moving closer to the confines of a particular tradition of critical discourse about imaginative literature that will help him see more clearly what he is about in *The Lord of the Rings*. He moves in the direction given him by the word *Faërie*; indeed for Tolkien the very wind that blows through the Perilous Realm is the spirit of mythology. He uses the same phrases in 1936 and 1938 to describe the difficulties in dealing with the two analytically. Just as myth is man's one imaginative act "capable . . . of becoming largely significant — as a whole, accepted unanalyzed" ("Monsters and Critics," p. 63), so is Faërie impermeable to analysis: "I will not attempt to define that, nor to describe it directly. It cannot be done. Faërie cannot be caught in a net of words; for it is one of its qualities to be indescribable, though not imperceptible. It has many ingredients, but analysis will not necessarily discover the secret of the whole" (TL, p. 10). So rather than describe, Tolkien attempts to place. Fantasy is not so much about elves or fairies, as about a "perilous land" (TL, p. 3), "about Fairy, that is *Faërie*, the realm or state in which fairies have their being. *Faërie* contains many things besides elves and fays, and besides dwarfs, witches, trolls, giants, or dragons: it holds the seas, the sun, the moon, the sky; and the earth, and all things that are in it: tree and bird, water and stone, wine and bread, and ourselves, mortal men, when we are enchanted" (TL, p. 9). In defining what he means by the sort of "realm" we are in when enchanted, Tolkien moves to the heart of one of the most venerable of our critical traditions, the one that sees the work of art as "heterocosm."[4]

In order, that is, to work out for himself critically what he is doing in *The Lord of the Rings*, Tolkien attaches his thinking to the strength of an ancient tradition, a not unusual tactic for the practitioner of a mode like romance. He makes the attachment with his notion of the "sub-creation" of a "Secondary World" and does it by way of a disagreement with Coleridge, the most famous member of that tradition. Tolkien argues that Coleridge's phrase "willing suspension of disbelief" "does not seem . . . a good description of what happens. What really happens is that the story-maker proves a successful 'sub-creator.' He makes a Secondary World which your mind can enter. Inside it, what he relates is 'true': it accords with the laws of that world. You therefore believe it, while you are, as it were, inside" (TL, p. 37). The artistic skill that places you in another world evokes the positive rather than negative state of Secondary Belief, "the enchanted state" (TL, p. 37).

The critical idea that a successful story-maker is creating another world, a heterocosm, probably found its first formal statement in fifteenth-century Florence. Cristoforo Landino, for example, in his commentary on Dante, wrote that

> the Greeks say "poet" from the verb "piin" [sic], which is halfway between "creating," which is peculiar to God when out of nothing he brings forth anything into being, and "making," which applies to men when they compose with matter and form in any art. It is for this reason that, although the feigning of the poet is not entirely out of nothing, it nevertheless departs from making and comes very near to creating. And God is the supreme poet, and the world is his poem.[5]

Landino is being very careful to avoid blasphemy. The poet,

he says, comes "very near" to creating, but never quite performs the divine act itself. Landino coyly reverses the direction of his metaphor at the end; rather than continue the thrust of his figure and say that the poet is divine, he turns it around and calls God poet. It remained for another age, and another poet, to insist that "The Eternal Body of Man is the Imagination, that is God himself the Divine Body . . . It manifests itself in his Works of Art" (as Blake says in *The Laocoön*). Standing between Landino and Blake are the essays that domesticated this sort of thinking into the English critical tradition and that probably stand directly behind Tolkien's own essay — Joseph Addison's series of *Spectator* papers "On the Pleasures of the Imagination," in June and July 1712. Borrowing a term from Dryden, Addison begins his own essay on fairy stories:

> There is a kind of writing, wherein the poet quite loses sight of nature and entertains his reader's imagination with the characters and actions of such persons as have many of them no existence, but what he bestows on them. Such are fairies, witches, magicians, demons, and departed spirits. This Mr. Dryden calls "the fairy way of writing," which is, indeed, more difficult than any other that depends on the poet's fancy, because he has no pattern to follow in it, and must work altogether out of his own invention.[6]

Tolkien echoes that the achievement of a successful fairy story "will probably require labour and thought, and will certainly demand a special skill, a kind of elvish craft. Few attempt such difficult tasks" (TL, p. 49). Addison observed that the fairy way of writing "makes additions to nature, and gives a greater variety to God's works."[7] Tolkien echoes that the fantasist "may actually assist in the effoliation and multiple enrichment of creation" (TL, p. 73). Regardless of whether or not Tolkien actually had Addison in his mind as he wrote, it is clear what he is attempting to do — reinvigorate the traditional notion of the poem as heterocosm, the story-maker as "secondary creator." Perhaps the clearest statement of the critical conception of fairy story as Secondary World before Tolkien's Lang Lecture, and which he must surely have known, is in Richard Hurd's eighteenth-century work, *Letters on Chivalry and Romance*: "A poet, they say, must follow *Nature*; and by Nature we are to suppose can only be meant the known and experienced course of affairs in this world. Whereas the poet has a world of his own, where experience has less to do, than consistent imagination." [8]

The poet makes "a world of his own." Sub-creation, then, as an "aspect of mythology" (TL, p. 23), is not to be taken lightly, Tolkien argues from his new position inside an old critical tradition. With some sarcasm, he notes that Andrew Lang, the man honored in the lecture he is delivering, said, "and is by some still commended for saying, that mythology and religion (in the strict sense of that word) are two distinct things that have become inextricably entangled, though mythology is in itself almost devoid of religious significance." But in fact, it is quite the other way around: "maybe they were sundered long ago and have since groped slowly, through a labyrinth of error, through confusion, back towards re-fusion" (TL, pp. 25–26). This is so, he urges, because the myth-making act of sub-creation, the creation in narrative literature of a Secondary World, is man's most godlike act: *"We make still by the law in which we're made"*; "we make in our measure and in our derivative mode, because we are made: and not only made, but made in the image and likeness of a Maker" (TL, pp. 54, 55). Therefore, precisely because "Something really 'higher' is occasionally glimpsed in mythology: Divinity" itself, it can work immensely important effects upon the reader (TL, p. 25). It is "small wonder," Tolkien remarks, "that *spell* means both a story told, and a formula of power over living men" (TL, p. 31).

Precisely what the "power" of fantasy is Tolkien explains in terms that are to a considerable extent personal, for of course the theory of Faërie he is developing in the Lang Lecture holds much more than an academic interest for him, caught as he is under its spell himself. "I have been a lover of fairy stories since I learned to read," he remarks in the opening paragraph, and continues this personal tone to the end. But it is not Tolkien's point that fairy stories are valuable to us now because he, or any other child, enjoyed them in the nursery. Fantasy is richly valuable, he is coming to understand through his own creation of one of the best examples of the genre, both for what it has always done for the adult imagination and for its peculiar benefits *now*, in a specific cultural situation. "Fairy-stories were plainly not primarily concerned with possibility, but with desirability. If they awakened *desire*, satisfying it while often whetting it unbearably, they succeeded . . ., this desire [is] a complex of many ingredients, some universal, some particular to modern men" (TL, p. 40). The universal desires are several, and, Tolkien says, primordial: "to hold communion with other living things," to "survey the depths of space and time" (TL, p. 13), and to explore "strange languages, and glimpses of an archaic mode of life, and, above all, forests" (TL, pp. 40–41). It is, of course, no accident that all these are central features in the narrative of *The Lord of the Rings* —

Treebeard, the First, Second, and Third Ages, the languages of the Orcs, Ents, and Elves, the forests of Fangorn and Mirkwood. Finally, "the primal desire at the heart of *Faërie* [is] the realization, independent of the conceiving mind, of imagined wonder" (TL, p. 14), "the making or glimpsing of Other-worlds" (TL, p. 41). All these have been functions of fantasy since the beginning of language, but, Tolkien continues, "what, if any, are the values and functions of fairy-stories *now?*" (TL, p. 33). The answers he gives relate directly to the overcoming of the imaginative poverty he saw behind his contemporaries' failure to respond to the mythological vision of *Beowulf.* Tolkien has not, of course, been the first to recognize the shocking, historically almost unique poverty of imaginative and mythic experience in our culture. He has the honored example of Matthew Arnold forlornly telling an increasingly secular Victorian world that poetry would come to replace religion as its chief source of imaginative enrichment but a source that could never be as widespread or as satisfyingly available as religion; and the more forlorn (because even less heeded) example of William Blake, trying to convince a pre-Victorian world that "Christianity is Art" (*The Laocoön*). Tolkien's profoundly suggestive insights into the sacral nature of the human imagination parallel Blake's rather than Arnold's, though he will not go quite so far as Blake in his claims for its divinity. The poetry of the mythic imagination will not, for Tolkien, *replace* religion so much as *make it possible,* putting imaginatively starved modern man back once again into awed and reverent contact with a living universe.

Tolkien calls the peculiar modern functions of fantasy "Recovery, Escape and Consolation." The first has to do directly with the health of the human imagination. "Recovery

(which includes return and renewal of health) is a re-gaining
— re-gaining of a clear view ... We need ... to clean our
windows; so that the things seen clearly may be freed from
the drab blur of triteness or familiarity" (TL, p. 57). Like
all Romantic artists, Tolkien is strongly convinced of the
instrumental priority of imagination over perception, that,
as Blake puts it, "we see *through*, not with the eye." Precisely
what enables us to see the real meaning or glory of our world
is the mythological imagination. As Tolkien's friend C. S.
Lewis said in a review of *The Lord of the Rings* about the
things of our experience, "By dipping them in myth we see
them more clearly." Just as graphically, Tolkien declares
that "By the forging of Gram cold iron was revealed; by
the making of Pegasus horses were ennobled; in the Trees
of the Sun and Moon root and stock, flower and fruit are
manifested in glory." Tolkien feels strongly that in our time
we need the gift of recovery as never before; in our Sauron-
esque delusions we have imagined too long that the world
is ours, that nature is our slave rather than our quiet master.
In the salutary experience of mythic Recovery "you will be
warned that all you had (or knew) was dangerous and potent,
not really effectively chained, free and wild; no more yours
than they were you" (TL, p. 59).

Escape, the second modern function of fantasy, is, Tolkien
quickly points out, not the "Flight of the Deserter" but the
"Escape of the Prisoner" (TL, p. 60), a desire compounded
of what might well be described as the peculiar modern
emotions, "Disgust, Anger, Condemnation and Revolt,"
against what he calls the "Robot Age" (TL, p. 61), an age
"out of touch with the life of nature and of human nature
as well" (TL, p. 64, quoting Christopher Dawson). "It is part
of the essential malady of such days — producing the desire

to escape, not indeed from life, but from our present time and self-made misery — that we are acutely conscious both of the ugliness of our works, and of their evil" (TL, pp. 64–65). Because of this "essential malady" at the heart of our culture, "Escape is one of the main functions of fairy-stories" (TL, p. 60). Fantasy would provide a healthy escape, closely related to Recovery, back into the full imaginative apprehension of real or natural things. Too much of our life and our art, Tolkien complains, is like "play under a glass roof by the side of a municipal swimming-bath" (TL, p. 63), forgetful of heaven and the sea. Escape would allow a *real* Recovery: "We should look at green again, and be startled anew (but not blinded) by blue and yellow and red. We should meet the centaur and the dragon, and then perhaps suddenly behold, like the ancient shepherds, sheep, and dogs, and horses — and wolves" (TL, p. 57).

The first two effects of fantasy are rather simple in their power and could probably be wrought by any effective art. The third, however, is for Tolkien of such significance that he can only describe it in metaphors of religious experience, placing it with the noblest of the genres, tragedy itself. Just as the purgation of tragedy is "the true form of Drama, its highest function," so the "opposite is true of Fairy-story," whose function is the "Consolation of the Happy Ending" (to which he gives the name *Eucatastrophe*), which can bring a "sudden and miraculous grace" that is in fact "*evangelium*, giving a fleeting glimpse of Joy, Joy beyond the walls of the world" (TL, p. 68). Tolkien means that at certain moments fantasy can so affect the spirit that it is put suddenly in touch with a deeper reality; fantasy can give what is in effect indistinguishable from religious experience, can give a "far-off gleam or echo of *evangelium* in the real world" (TL,

p. 71). By thus redefining the effects of fairy stories, Tolkien has given a new validity to the study and appreciation of mythological literature (not least his own), opening it up to richer understanding of its power. He has, for example, created a completely new tool for the study of the Gospels as fantasy literature; for, he says, they "contain a fairy-story, or a story of a larger kind which embraces all the essence of fairy-stories" (TL, p. 71). The rich audacity of this remark is a clear sign that Tolkien the Roman Catholic has achieved a real imaginative breakthrough in this essay, has earned a release that will go far toward thawing the hard winter of 1938–1939. At any rate he has worked out for himself in the Lang Lecture a coherent theory of fantasy, and an insight parallel to Blake's that "Christianity is Art." He has grasped clearly the affective functions of fantasy literature, asserting that it can give a "joy that [has] exactly the same quality, if not the same degree," as the "Christian joy, the *Gloria*" felt by every Christian with each new experiencing of what Tolkien calls the "eucatastrophe of the story of the Incarnation" — Easter (TL, p. 72). For the Christian reader at least, Tolkien declares, fantasy "Art has been verified" by the Gospel, which has "not abrogated legends [but] has hallowed them" (TL, p. 73).

TOLKIEN'S LEAF

The Hobbit *and*
the Discovery of a World

It had begun with a leaf caught in the wind, and it became
a tree; and the tree grew, sending out innumerable
branches, and thrusting out the most fantastic roots.
Strange birds came and settled on the twigs and had to
be attended to. Then all round the Tree, and behind it,
through the gaps in the leaves and boughs, a country began
to open out; and there were glimpses of a forest marching
over the land, and of mountains tipped with snow.

— TOLKIEN, "Leaf by Niggle"

THE STORY of Tolkien's world begins with *The Hobbit*,
but we may founder on this book unless we grasp that
it is for children and filled with a whimsy few adults can
accept with pleasure. A year after the publication of his
children's story, Tolkien stated a wisdom hard won: "If
fairy-story as a kind is worth reading at all it is worthy to
be written for and read by adults" (TL, p. 45). He had to
write *The Hobbit* in order to learn this truth and then the
essay "On Fairy-Stories," here quoted, to work out critically
what the discovery meant. Perhaps hardest of all was the
painful lesson that *The Hobbit* was, for the writer who wanted
seriously to explore the fairy story's immense possibilities
for imaginative discovery, aimed wrong, childish. Yet para-

doxically, he would not even have learned of those possibilities without the maturing experience of his first attempt and
of thinking through its implications. For the fact is, *The Hobbit*
taught Tolkien how to write *The Lord of the Rings* and then
forced him to complete it. In his children's story he discovered his theme, learned what he had to say and how the
fairy story could say it; captured by that theme, he was drawn
irresistibly into a world that would make it credible. Tolkien
himself has testified to the daunting labors lying behind such
a discovery in words clearly picturing his own combination
of pleasure and dissatisfaction with *The Hobbit* and his desire
to continue its mode in another work. Writing in 1938, a
year after the publication of *The Hobbit* and a time when
he was already well into the first book of *The Lord of the
Rings,* he said that fantasy

> is and has been used frivolously, or only half-
> seriously, or merely for decoration: it remains
> merely "fanciful." Anyone inheriting the fantastic
> device of human language can say *the green sun.*
> Many can then imagine or picture it. But that is
> not enough — though it may already be a more
> potent thing than many a "thumbnail sketch" or
> "transcript of life" that receives literary praise.
>
> To make a Secondary World inside which the
> green sun will be credible, commanding Secondary
> Belief, will probably require labour and thought,
> and will certainly demand a special skill, a kind
> of elvish craft (TL, pp. 48–49).

With *The Hobbit* Tolkien had said *the green sun,* but frivolously,
or at least whimsically. With *The Lord of the Rings* (already
in progress) the green sun would be made credible with a

world, and a conception, in keeping with the audacity of the invention. And this is indeed what happened, for we have in *The Hobbit* and its sequel what is in fact the same story, told first very simply, and then again, very intricately. Both works have the same theme, a quest on which a most unheroic hobbit achieves heroic stature; they have the same structure, the "there and back again" of the quest romance, and both extend the quest through the cycle of one year, *The Hobbit* from spring to spring, the *Rings* from fall to fall.

The episodic structures of the two books are so closely parallel one says without exaggeration that *The Lord of the Rings* is *The Hobbit* writ large. Both begin in festivity (the "Unexpected Party" in Chapter I of the first, the "Long-Expected Party" in Chapter I of the sequel) and continue with lengthy scenes of initiating information (about Smaug and the treasure, about Sauron and the Ring). In both works this information precipitates the heroes' unhobbitlike decisions to leave the Shire on a perilous journey, the first leg of which will take both to Rivendell. On the way, each undergoes frightening but sobering adventures and grows considerably in heroic stature, acquiring a sword in an unexpected way and later using it in most unhobbitlike fashion (Bilbo attacking the spiders of Mirkwood, Frodo the Barrow-wight). On reaching the Last Homely House, both hobbits rest, recuperate, and decide what to do next, decisions involving in each case a conference with Elrond the Elf-Lord. Soon after leaving Rivendell, replete with advice and provisions, both hobbits must pass the treacherous Misty Mountains. In both works, a storm prevents the travelers' progress over the passes, and in both, their next move is to enter a cave. Here, the heroes are threatened by Orcs and encounter Gollum for the first time (Bilbo in the riddle game,

Frodo when he hears Gollum's softly padding feet in Moria). During the underground encounter, the members of the two companies are separated (Bilbo from Gandalf and the dwarves, Frodo and the Walkers from Gandalf after his combat with the Balrog). From this point in both works, the hero must proceed without the help of the wizard (though Bilbo's long separation from Gandalf does not begin until after the encounter with Beorn in Chapter VII).

Bilbo's meeting with Beorn occurs in the middle of his first sequence of adventures, as does its parallel in the *Rings,* Frodo's encounter with Tom Bombadil. Both Beorn and Tom are in some way "nature spirits," able to merge with and control nature at will — Tom addresses and controls the trees of Old Forest, Beorn does the same with the creatures of his domain and as a "skin changer" can become a bear. In both initiating contacts with the spirit of nature, the hobbits learn of the wiles and duplicity of the great forest and of nature in general: Tom tells of Old Man Willow and the lesser trees of Old Forest, Beorn of Mirkwood and its dark secrets.

In both books the initial sequence of adventures preparing the hero for his great quest ends with a trip down a river to the edge of the territory of the evil power whose defeat is the object of the story. And in each book the hero, in reaching his final climactic adventure, must cross the blasted land surrounding the center of evil, reach and ascend a mountain, enter it by a hole in its side, and so entering discover the one vulnerable spot in the defenses of the evil — Smaug's unprotected side, Sauron's dependence on the power of the Ring.

Following the success of the quest, both works see a purging of Middle-earth in a great battle — the Battle of Five Armies in *The Hobbit*, of Morannon Gate in its sequel, each climaxing with the arrival of a great flight of eagles signaling the victory of the hero's side. At the height of each battle, the hero suddenly disappears when he puts on the Ring while standing on a hill or mountain (though Frodo is of course at Mount Doom, not at Morannon). After vanishing, both hobbits are wounded (Bilbo by a blow on the head, Frodo by Gollum's teeth) and faint away, awakening to news of complete victory. But in both works, joy of victory is tempered by report of the death of a king who redeemed his former ill deeds in a heroic charge against the enemy (Kings Thorin and Théoden). Finally, after the full recognition of the heroes, each takes the long journey homeward, parting along the way with various friends. Reaching Hobbiton, both find they have been dispossessed in their absence and must exert themselves one last time to regain Bag End, the ancestral home. Having done so, both halflings settle down, but neither ever regains the trust or understanding of his neighbors, remaining instead closely friendly with a small circle of hobbits, a great number of elves and dwarves, and with Gandalf. In the end, both leave Hobbiton to spend their last long years with elves, Bilbo retiring (in the *Rings*) to Rivendell, Frodo to the Uttermost West.

But if *The Hobbit* and *The Lord of the Rings* are in essence the "same book," why did Tolkien feel obliged to write again what he had already done once? The answer is, of course, that far from being the same book, they have merely the same narrative husk; between them is a host of subtle and profound differences. In the writing of *The Hobbit* Tolkien learned more about himself, and about the imagination's frightening power and autonomy, than he would have thought possible in, say, 1930. The "leaf" called *The Hobbit* grew under his hand and almost against his will into a world too various and intriguing to leave unexplored; the leaf became a tree, and the tree a country, encircled with great and mysterious mountains. Tolkien had to *see* those mountains, so even before *The Hobbit* was published he was at work on its sequel, a work in which Middle-earth has undergone a wondrous sea change.

Tolkien himself has considered the critical problem of the "same story" existing in different forms in a passage that could well relate to this very likeness between his two tales:

> To investigators of this sort [folklore scholars] recurring similarities . . . seem especially important. So much so that students of folk-lore are apt to get off their own proper track, or to express themselves in a misleading "shorthand" . . . They are inclined to say that any two stories that are built around the same folk-lore motive, or are made up of a generally similar combination of such motives, are "the same stories" . . .
>
> Statements of that kind may express (in undue abbreviation) some element of truth; but they are not true in a fairy-story sense, they are not true in art or literature. It is precisely the colouring, the atmosphere, the unclassifiable individual details of a story, and above all the general purport that informs with life the undissected bones of the plot, that really count (TL, pp. 18–19).

Here precisely are the differences between *The Hobbit* and the *Rings*, for despite the similarities between them, the first is in all respects *smaller* than its sequel, in direct proportion as the readers of the one are smaller than the readers of the other. In the earlier work, Tolkien is addressing children and dealing with a closely limited theme — growing up — telling about Bilbo's "birth" out of Bag End and his gradual initiation into full "manhood." Tolkien's moral is little more than "Be brave, enter life's dark secret places; there may be golden treasure hid within." *The Hobbit* is, at its narrative heart, a book about entering and grasping, and taking forth symbols of manhood. Again and again, Bilbo must enter a forbidden place guarded closely by a figure of terror or power, and steal something precious: the troll's purse (and gold and sword), Gollum's ring, the spiders' dwarf-prey, the elf-king's prisoners, Smaug's cup, Thorin's Arkenstone. It is no accident that Bilbo's title is "burglar"; he is adept at sneaking, hiding, finding secret entrances and exits — after all, his chief use of the Ring will be to avoid nuisances like the Sackville-Bagginses. In other words, the moral elements of *The Hobbit* are relatively simple, something evident to any adult reader, and really no damning criticism of a children's book; what is striking is the contrast to its sequel — a story grown vastly greater in import and application, heavy with the fate of civilizations and the weight of long history.

The moral smallness of *The Hobbit* in comparison to its sequel is clear from the beginning. Both heroes decide in the second chapter of their stories they will leave the Shire and begin a quest, but the natures of the two quests and the reasons for beginning them are strikingly different. Bilbo's is at first little more than a lark with venal motives (a share in Smaug's treasure), and his initial decision to join the dwarves is simply a matter of Tookish pride; he had shrieked and fainted at the first hint he "may never return" from an encounter with Smaug and was carried into the next room. But on hearing Gandalf's assurance that he is "fierce as a dragon in a pinch," and Glóin's demurrer that he "looks

more like a grocer than a burglar," Bilbo's pride flares up:
"He suddenly felt he would go without bed and breakfast
to be thought fierce." [1] Finally, Bilbo's leaving Bag End on
his adventures is more the result of Gandalf's fast talking
than of Bilbo's own deciding.

> "But —," said Bilbo.
> "No time for it," said the wizard.
> "But —," said Bilbo again.
> "No time for that either! Off you go!"
> To the end of his days Bilbo could never remember
> how he found himself outside, without a hat, a
> walking-stick or any money (pp. 38–39).

When Frodo leaves Bag End, however, he goes with the
pain of a sad but noble decision, bearing with him the fate
of an entire world. He has just learned that Bilbo's magic
toy is in fact the One Ring of Power, source of enough wicked
potency to control all of Middle-earth, and that Sauron, its
maker, is seeking it desperately. Frodo sees, consequently,
that "I am a danger, a danger to all that live near me. I
cannot keep the Ring and stay here. I ought to leave Bag
End, leave the Shire, leave everything and go away" (I,
p. 71).

Tolkien in *The Lord of the Rings* tells the "same story,"
but as he said in 1938, the "atmosphere" and "general
purport" make a great difference. In the earlier work, com-
posed for his children, he adopts an "angle of address" of
approximately forty-five degrees, talking down to his little
listeners; this stance controls the tone, as in the opening
paragraph: "In a hole in the ground there lived a hobbit.
Not a nasty, dirty, wet hole, filled with the ends of worms
and an oozy smell." This first page, and indeed much of

the book, is marred for the adult reader by a set of tonal quirks, perhaps the worst being the excessive number of modifiers — "perfectly," "very," "lots and lots," "on and on," "many," "little" (all from the first page) — and the frequent authorial intrusiveness, clearly taken over in imitation of oral storytelling style in which a narrator (Daddy at bedtime) breaks in to share private jokes with his diminutive listeners: "Yes, I am afraid trolls do behave like that, even those with only one head each" (p. 44).

Corollary to the tone of the early parts of *The Hobbit* is an obvious lack of moral inclusiveness, a narrowing of the range of good and evil permissible to its characters. There is a clear difference in moral depth, for example, between the initial adventures of Bilbo and Frodo on the road to Rivendell. Bilbo's adventures begin on the night of June 1. Inexplicably separated from Gandalf, the dwarves and the hobbit find themselves cold and supperless on a wet night, grimly preparing to sleep on the ground, when they spy a light ahead. Bilbo the burglar, sent forward to reconnoiter, discovers trolls, fierce, man-eating creatures, on a raiding expedition. But such trolls! "Mutton yesterday, mutton today, and blimey, if it don't look like mutton again tomorrer . . . Yer can't expect folk to stop here for ever just to be et by you and Bert. You've et a village and a half between yer, since we come down from the mountains" (p. 44). Tolkien deliberately undercuts the force of our response to the trolls' wickedness by giving them a Cockney dialect, and a rather crudely presented one at that. We are asked to laugh as well as shudder, and caught between the two reactions, we finally have neither. But this is, of course, the adult response; what Tolkien has done with his trolls is altogether suitable for children, and there is no use in faulting him for undercutting the evil. The tone is at one with the substance of the scene and with the minds of the audience. All we can say here is that Tolkien has not yet purged himself of the notion of a natural connection between fairy stories and the minds of children, has yet to learn that, as he wrote a year after publishing *The Hobbit*, "Fairy-stories banished in this way [to the nursery], cut off from a full adult art, would in the end be ruined" (TL, p. 35). One of the results of writing *The Hobbit* would be Tolkien's learning this truth.

Compare, now, Bilbo's trolls with the account of Frodo's first adventure on the way to Elrond's. Again separated inexplicably from Gandalf, and again on the road at night, the hobbit and his companions trudge toward Rivendell. Suddenly hearing hoofbeats, they hide beside the road:

> As Frodo watched he saw something dark pass across the lighter space between two trees, and then halt. It looked like the black shade of a horse led by a smaller black shadow. The black shadow . . . swayed from side to side. Frodo thought he heard the sound of snuffling. The shadow bent to the ground, and then began to crawl towards him (I, p. 88).

The jocular authorial intrusiveness has disappeared, and the evil is distilled to its mythic and elemental basis — shadow — lacking not only a comic dialect, but even the humanizing force of speech itself. The hero faces not comic villains, but something wholly inexplicable, against which he has no defense at all — the stuff of bad dreams, perhaps, but essential fantasy.

Just as evil is undercut in *The Hobbit*, so is good. When Bilbo arrives at Rivendell, he finds not the exalted and

mysterious elves of the *Rings*, but gay and chattering Little
People, eager to tease and joke, lacking in all but the power
to amuse. In the children's version of Tolkien's story, the
elven-folk sing delicious nonsense, gay and carefree:

O! What are you doing,
And where are you going?
Your ponies need shoeing!
The river is flowing!
O! tra-la-la-lally
here down in the valley!

. . . .

O! tril-lil-lil-lolly
the valley is jolly,
ha! ha! (p. 58).

The elves of the *Rings* are another order of creature entirely.
They too are first heard singing, but the song has deepened,
turned melancholy with the weight of years and ancient
sadness, though still beautiful, for to Tolkien elves are the
pre-eminently imaginative folk, who above all others have
the enchanting power of beauty:

Gilthoniel! O Elbereth!
Clear are thy eyes and bright thy breath!
Snow-white! Snow-white! We sing to thee
In a far land beyond the Sea.

. . . .

O Elbereth! Gilthoniel!
We still remember, we who dwell
In this far land beneath the trees,
Thy starlight on the Western Seas (I, pp. 88–89).

Tolkien is not quite poet enough in these verses to convince
us irrevocably of the beauty of elvish song, but it is clear,

at least, what he is trying to do. The beauty of the elves' utterance is to be the objective correlative for their goodness, even as the ugliness of the Dark Tongue (*Ash nazg durbatulûk*) will express the inner rot of Sauron. But there is no hint of such an idea in *The Hobbit*; we are still in a children's world — delightful though it be for many readers — a world yet to be touched with a genuine sense of evil, or even of overarching goodness. *The Hobbit*, in other words, lacks a certain intellectual weight, lacks the commitment, fully expressed in *The Lord of the Rings*, to exploring and revealing the enriching, ennobling functions of fantasy. That commitment is on the verge of being made somewhere in the latter part of *The Hobbit*, and it achieves full critical statement in "On Fairy-Stories," where Tolkien declares that the enchantment of *Faërie* is the elves' best work, bringing with it Recovery, Escape, and Consolation.

Tolkien's clearest narrative statement of the enchanting, transporting power of elvish art comes in the second book of the *Rings*, in the passage parallel to that telling of Bilbo's arrival at Rivendell. In *The Hobbit* the narrator intrudes directly after the first elvish song to comment self-consciously on the silliness of it all:

> So they laughed and sang in the trees; and pretty fair nonsense I daresay you think it. Not that they would care; they would only laugh all the more if you told them so. They were elves of course . . .
> Then off they went into another song as ridiculous as the one I have written down in full (p. 59).

In the sequel, the narrator eschews direct commentary and instead slips inside Frodo's head to describe the enchanted, heightened state created by elvish music:

At first the beauty of the melodies and the inter-
woven words in the Elven-tongue, even though he
understood them little, held him in a spell, as soon
as he began to attend to them. Almost it seemed
that the words took shape, and visions of far lands
and bright things that he had never yet imagined
opened out before him (I, p. 245).

In *The Hobbit*, Tolkien is not yet ready for such a full-scale
realization of the enchanting power of elves; he can only
apologize that "I wish I had time to tell you even a few
of the tales or one or two of the songs that they heard in
that house" (p. 61).

After leaving Rivendell, the travelers must in both books
proceed eastward, over the Misty Mountains. Again they
encounter wicked creatures, but again in *The Hobbit* their
wickedness is undercut by comedy, for there they are called
Goblins, a name that summons little more to the imagination
than childish pranks at Halloween. "Now goblins are cruel,
wicked, and bad-hearted" (p. 73), Tolkien tells us, but his
chief way of showing their mischief is to make them sing
a comic-patter song about pinching and yammering:

> *Clap! Snap! the black crack!*
> *Grip, grab! Pinch, nab!*
> *And down down to Goblin-town*
>   *You go, my lad!*
>
> *Clash, crash! Crush, smash!*
> *Hammer and tongs! Knocker and gongs!*
> *Pound, pound, far underground!*
>   *Ho, ho! my lad!*
>
> *Swish, smack! Whip crack!*
> *Batter and beat! Yammer and bleat!*

Work, work! Nor dare to shirk,
While Goblins quaff, and Goblins laugh,
Round and round far underground
Below, my lad (pp. 71–72).

This, we are told, "sounded truly terrifying" (p. 72). But of course it isn't terrifying at all, nor does Tolkien intend it to be so; these Goblins are not the Orcs of the *Rings*, even though they are "in fact" the same creatures, since "Orc" is the Gondolin word for the race called "Goblins" in the Hobbit tongue.

What, then, is the deepening impulse, where the magic moment, when Tolkien's vision begins to probe and plumb, touching at last richness and complexity? As we should expect, it begins when Tolkien's hero encounters Middle-earth's most compelling symbol, the Ring, and its most complex and engaging creature, that strange hobbit called Gollum. Almost, one could say, as soon as Gollum and the Ring appear, *The Lord of the Rings* is inevitable, for the two stimulate and deepen Tolkien's imagination, in the direction of a complex Secondary World, more than any other of the inventions in *The Hobbit*. With Gollum and the Ring is the beginning of Tolkien's exploration of the puzzlement and fascination of evil; with Gollum especially, Tolkien has hit upon his most complex representative figure of the satanic in Middle-earth, and one that will grow very quickly in his imagination into the never-seen title figure of *The Lord of the Rings*, Sauron the Great. Sauron, like Gollum, is a figure of immense age, once not evil to behold, who has lost something of incalculable importance to him and whose life's object is to get it back again. Clearly the distant but still recognizable model for Sauron (and even Gollum) is Milton's

Satan, likewise a creature of immense age and former beauty, who has lost heaven and must forever seek to regain it, but just as clearly the imaginative transformation of the model has been very great.[2] For reasons somewhat like those behind Milton's never directly representing God (we see only His eye and hand), Tolkien never directly represents Sauron (again, we see only his eye and hand). With immense modesty and perspicuity, Tolkien has recognized the limits of his rich but narrow genius and keeps Sauron in the background, a hovering and unimaginable symbol of irredeemable evil, and gives us in the foreground only a worm's-eye view of wickedness, Sauron's wretched servant Gollum, who also has lost the precious Ring, and must again find it or be forever gnawed by its desire.

But of course Tolkien grasps nothing of this in the early 1930s, when he writes of Bilbo's encounter with Gollum: "I don't know where he came from, nor who or what he was. He was Gollum — as dark as darkness" (p. 82). Yet only a matter of months passed before the discovery of Gollum and the Ring prodded Tolkien's imagination into a full working-out of their story. It is hardly too much to say that Gollum and the Ring are the central figures in the history of the unraveling of *The Lord of the Rings* in Tolkien's imagination, the roots that fed the imaginative growth of Middle-earth from leaf to cosmos. The possibilities of a device like the Ring must have struck Tolkien like a blow. What are the moral implications of owning a ring of invisibility? In what sort of world, with what fictional laws, could such a ring exist? Who might make it? What would he be like? Filled with such intriguing questions, Tolkien's imagination set about building a world within which his "green sun" would be credible. Even before *The Hobbit* appeared in print,

Tolkien, spurred by the discovery of the Ring, was writing
the connecting link between that book and its much greater
sequel, writing, in the second chapter of *The Lord of the Rings*,
the story of Gollum and his Precious. This is probably the
earliest written chapter of the story ("one of the oldest parts
of the tale" [I, p. 6], Tolkien wrote in the Foreword to *The
Fellowship*), "begun soon after *The Hobbit* was written and
before its publication in 1937" (I, p. 5). In this chapter Gandalf
tells Frodo all he knows of the Ring's and Gollum's histories,
and it is here that "ring" first becomes "Ring" (I, p. 59),
that "the Necromancer" (nameless, vague, and unmenacing)
becomes "Sauron," and that the cozy world of Bilbo suddenly
becomes older, and darker, and immeasurably more potent.

With the writing of the second chapter of the *Rings*, Tolkien
summoned something immensely larger than *The Hobbit* — an
entire world with its own history and perilous future, for
in telling the story of Gollum and the Ring, he began seriously
to invent the long history of Middle-earth. As Gandalf tells
it (and as the chronology in III, pp. 368, 373 dates it), five
hundred and fifty-five years before the recounting of the
narrative of that second chapter, Déagol the Stoor found the
One Ring. It had lain in the River Anduin, unseen and
forgotten by all but Sauron, for 2461 years, but immediately
upon Déagol's discovery, its evil effects begin again. Déagol's
friend, Sméagol, seeing it and loving its beauty, strangles
him and steals the lovely thing. Immediately touched by
its evil, Sméagol becomes an invisible thief, earns the ugly
name Gollum, and grows to hate the light of the sun and
the sight of his fellows. He hides under the Misty Mountains
for four hundred and seventy-eight years, until Bilbo, lost
in the goblin-caves, finds his Ring, and begins a new chapter
in its history. Bilbo is touched by the Ring according to

his nature and is moved to lie about how he got it but is otherwise unaffected except that he grows no older. Gandalf explains that because Bilbo gained the Ring with pity and mercy (rather than the murder with which Gollum took it) the Ring's evil only faintly corrupted him, while the good effects of his action made it possible for Frodo to inherit the Ring and begin his own quest for its destruction. And thus begins *The Lord of the Rings*.

Even more important than Bilbo's reaction to the discovery of the One Ring is Tolkien's. He changes on discovering his central symbol, his imagination grows and deepens, and even *The Hobbit*, in its later parts, feels the effects of the discovery of the Ring; it remains a children's book, narrow in moral range, but the tone shifts, and a greater sense of the possibilities of good and evil seems to erupt from the underside of Tolkien's imagination. First of all, the frequent authorial intrusions that mar the early part of the book change to direct comments with a much flattened angle of address — the audience seems taller now: "I have never heard what happened to the chief of the guards and the butler" (p. 212); "Actually I may say he put on his ring early in the business [the Battle of Five Armies] and vanished from sight, if not from all danger" (p. 294).

One explanation for the tonal shift in *The Hobbit*, though far too simplistic to suffice, tells part of the truth. As in all books, form is, after all, content, style *is* substance, and a hobbit of the Shire, even one with Tookish blood, is, literally, the same height as the young audience of his story (three feet, sometimes approaching four), and until he grows in metaphoric stature (and his growth is the theme of the story), puzzled disorientation *must* be called "flummoxed," and an angry curse *will* be mouthed as "confusticate and bebother." As Bilbo grows, so do Tolkien's style and imagination.

But even if we reject as fanciful the notion that the maturation of Tolkien's style is the objective correlative of Bilbo's growth to heroic stature, and even as we grant that a tonal shift is the sign of something more important than a developing technique, we must accept the obvious, that Tolkien did, somewhere about midpoint in the story, begin adjusting his tone with more skill. The first half of *The Hobbit* has only one tone — jocular down-talk — but the second becomes increasingly complex tonally. In Chapter I, for example, Thorin is capable only of comic verbosity: "We are met together in the house of our friend and fellow conspirator, this most excellent and audacious hobbit — may the hair on his toes never fall out" (pp. 24–25). But by the end, Tolkien has learned (or Thorin has grown) to express a wide range of tones, from a complex of pride and greed, to a dignified pathos:

> "For the Arkenstone of my father," he said, "is worth more than a river of gold in itself, and to me it is beyond price. That stone of all the treasure I name unto myself, and I will be avenged on anyone who finds it and withholds it" (p. 279).

> I go now to the halls of waiting [says the dying Thorin] to sit beside my fathers, until the world is renewed. Since I leave now all gold and silver, and go where it is of little worth, I wish to part in friendship from you (pp. 300–301).

But of course Thorin's real change is in his heart not his speech, and the change is a clear sign of Tolkien's deepening conception of the Middle-earth of the Ring. Tolkien's development as a prose stylist, Bilbo's growth toward heroic stature, Thorin's deepening character — here are the main, interrelated signs of the beginning of the depth and complexity of *The Lord of the Rings,* and the beginning as well of the one theme in *The Hobbit* with adult moral interest: the nature and meaning of power. (It is, of course, no accident that this is also a central theme in *The Hobbit*'s sequel.) It is, perhaps, a theme one would expect to find in any account of a fictional world, but it is one Tolkien only slowly grew toward. He had first to learn that a serious and important theme could be dealt with in a mythological narrative — in this case the theme was maturation. Next he learned, and again rather slowly, that serious themes could be dealt with in such a narrative *seriously* rather than whimsically or patronizingly. Then, at the end of *The Hobbit,* he learned one more lesson as he imaginatively explored the final growth and greatness of Thorin and Bilbo. He had to grasp the significance of the one great theme that differentiates the otherwise identical plot shells of the narratives of Bilbo and Frodo: the courageous renunciation of power. It is this theme that ennobles *The Lord of the Rings,* animating and supporting its far greater dignity and seriousness. For while both books are built upon the ancient structure of the quest, both concerned with the central plot of the maturation of an untried and apparently weak hero, they are differentiated in one great way: *The Hobbit* is a quest to *get* something, *The Lord of the Rings* a quest to *renounce* something. Tolkien is in the process of discovering that theme of renunciation in the final pages of his children's book. The minor expression of the theme in *The Hobbit* is Thorin's renunciation of his kingly pride and greed just before his death; the major expression is Bilbo's giving up the Arkenstone, an act directly foreshadowing Frodo's greatness in renouncing the Ring.

The theme of power (as opposed to its renunciation) attains prominence in *The Hobbit* in the very chapter describing the Ring's discovery; from this point the book's narrative rapidly develops away from its original motive of Bilbo's venal lark, as the Ring's effects begin to be felt. At first (and only tangentially, just before the Ring's discovery) with the Great Goblin, then with the Elvenking, then with the Master of Lake-Town, and finally, in the fullest way, with Thorin, Tolkien explores the social and moral ramifications of the actions of a greedy, self-seeking, and morally imperceptive leader (quite unknowingly preparing himself for his delineations of Denethor, Saruman, and Sauron). But this side of the "power" theme — to get rather than to renounce — relates only to the nonhobbit characters. Bilbo himself, to be sure, *began* that way — his quest was at first merely for a share in Smaug's treasure — but the Ring and its implications jolted Tolkien into an understanding of what hobbits were really for in Middle-earth, and with the episode of Bilbo and the Arkenstone comes at last Tolkien's (and Bilbo's) release into greatness — the first expression of his great and liberating theme and the discovery that will inspire twenty years of creative labor: Renunciation.

In Bilbo's great renunciation scene Tolkien's prose style (which is in most of the book the index of its failure as adult literature) works for the first time fully in his favor. Bilbo's speech is exactly, richly, delicately expressive of his character and the nature of his action; he is stiff and pompous but is that way precisely because he is embarrassed by his own recognition of the nobility of his action. The stiffness of his language is functional, exactly representative of his own self-discovery: "How can I, *I*, possibly be doing such a thing as this, stealing the most precious of all gems from the most unbendingly greedy of kings, and then giving it away to forestall a war?"

"Really, you know," Bilbo was saying in his best business manner, "things are impossible. Personally I am tired of the whole affair. I wish I was back in the West in my own home, where folk are more reasonable. But I have an interest in this matter — one fourteenth share, to be precise . . . A share in the *profits*, mind you," he went on. "I am aware of that. Personally I am only too ready to consider all your claims carefully, and deduct what is right from the total before putting in my own claim. However you don't know Thorin Oakenshield as well as I do now. I assure you, he is quite ready to sit on a heap of gold and starve, as long as you sit here."

"Well, let him!" said Bard. "Such a fool deserves to starve."

"Quite so," said Bilbo. "I see your point of view. At the same time winter is coming on fast. Before long you will be having snow and what not, and supplies will be difficult — even for elves I imagine" (pp. 282–83).

This last touch of sly diplomacy is Bilbo at his greatest; he is stiff and embarrassed, but he is anything but ridiculous. Gandalf's statement after Bilbo has given the Arkenstone to Bard might well echo Tolkien's own pleasure at the wonderful potentialities of these hobbits his imagination has summoned: "There is always more about you than anyone expects" (p. 285). Tolkien is justly pleased with his hobbit creations, and with their potential for realizing what he has discovered to be both his own great theme and their proper greatness, the spiritual power of renunciation.

> "Now I will make you an offer!"
> "Let us hear it!" they said.
> "You may see it!" said he. "It is this!" and he drew forth the Arkenstone, and threw away the wrapping (p. 283).

III

THE HOBBIT AS SWAIN
A World of Myth

To make the dream-story from which *Wonderland* was
elaborated seem Freudian one has only to tell it. A fall
through a deep hole into the secrets of Mother Earth
produces a new enclosed soul wondering who it is, what
will be its position in the world, and how it can get
out . . . Strange changes, caused by the way it is nourished
there, happen to it in this place, but always when it is
big it cannot get out and when it is small it is not allowed
to; for one thing, being a little girl, it has no key.

— WILLIAM EMPSON,
on *Alice in Wonderland*

I T MUST SEEM a curious thing that there has been so little
serious criticism of the hobbits. There is perhaps a feeling
that real criticism would involve psychoanalysis and that the
results would be so improper as to destroy the atmosphere
of the book altogether. Yet *The Hobbit* is so frankly about
growing up that there is no great discovery in translating
it into analytic terms; this seems indeed the only proper
exegesis of such a classic, even if it would be a shock to
the author.

To make the story of *The Hobbit* seem Freudian, one has
only to tell it. Before his adventures begin, Bilbo Baggins
dwells in a hobbit-hole with a round door, a home aptly
named Bag End — a bag with a round opening, the perfect

womb symbol. The round door "opened on to a tube-shaped hall like a tunnel," the vagina of Bag End. Inside is the ultimate in soft, womblike comfort: "panelled walls, and floors tiled and carpeted,... pantries (lots of those), wardrobes (he had whole rooms devoted to clothes), kitchens, dining-rooms" (p. 9). The owner of such a house wants the moist comforts of the embryo, so hobbits prefer dinner "twice a day when they can get it" (p. 10) and like to relax afterward with the hobbit version of thumb-sucking — smoking pipes, an art that Tolkien says they invented. Thus we first see Bilbo "standing at his door after breakfast smoking an enormous long wooden pipe" (p. 11), secure in his knowledge that Bagginses "never had any adventures." But of course *The Hobbit* is to be a "story of how a Baggins had an adventure, and found himself doing and saying things altogether unexpected" (p. 10). Before Bilbo can have his adventure, though, he must leave the soft comforts of Bag End and be symbolically "born" with all the helpless nakedness of the infant. And this is precisely what happens: "To the end of his days Bilbo could never remember how he found himself outside, without a hat, a walking-stick or any money" (pp. 38–39), or even a pocket handkerchief. Propelled by what seems a will other than his own, Bilbo finds himself "leaving his second breakfast half-finished," hurrying "down the lane, past the great Mill, across The Water" (p. 39) to Bywater to join the dwarves on their adventure. Now born and symbolically naked, he is ready to begin his pilgrimage toward the dragon's lair.

No longer an embryo but now an infant, Bilbo finds himself compelled to earn gradually his maturity, to acquire the symbols of his "manhood" and a secure sense of ego-identity. He must reach adulthood before he can encounter the dragon, and his first experience outside the womb of Bag End shows how far he has to go. On the road at night with his companions in a cold rain Bilbo sees a light ahead. Going forward to seek what we would expect — food and warmth — he finds trolls, fierce, man-eating creatures, on a lowland raiding expedition and attempts to pick the pocket of the nearest one (tries, quite without realizing it, to earn a phallus the easy way). The purse he grabs, however, turns out to be magical and fully aware that Bilbo is no man to carry a troll's purse: " 'Ere, 'oo are you?" it asks. Bilbo in response stammers, momentarily unsure of his own identity, "a bur — a hobbit" (p. 45). He is certainly no burglar yet, and, unless he can grow quickly, can hardly expect to remain long a hobbit either. Fortunately he does grow, and before the encounter with the trolls is over, Bilbo has taken his first large step toward identity and earned the first symbol of his heroic "manhood" — a small sword.

The dwarves, likewise, must undergo a distressing "birth," from the sacks in which the trolls have imprisoned them, before they may be fit companions for the hobbit. The trolls have grabbed Bilbo and are trying to decide how to cook him when the anxious dwarves come up one by one to see what is the matter, only to be caught and stuffed into "a nasty smelly sack" (p. 47). Bilbo later acts as midwife, helping Gandalf "untie the sacks and let out the dwarves" (p. 51). Now that all the members of the quest have achieved "birth," they are ready for the first of a sequence of adventures that will form the narrative backbone of *The Hobbit*: the hero must enter a dark, forbidding or forbidden place, usually through a tunnel, the entrance to which is guarded by a figure of power or terror, and bring forth persons important to the quest or an object heavy with symbolic implications.

This sequence begins at the trolls' cave. They "searched about," after the petrification of the wicked creatures, "and soon found the marks of trolls' stony boots going away through the trees. They followed the tracks up the hill, until hidden by bushes they came on a big door of stone leading to a cave" (p. 52). "Hidden by bushes" — the symbolic implications are probably unconscious on Tolkien's part but are clear enough to the analytic reader. But wait. The hobbit and his companions cannot enter; the door is locked. The forbidden cave, hidden behind its bushy covering and guarded by voracious trolls (now reduced to stone), can be entered only by him who owns the proper key, and who should have it but Bilbo! " 'Would this be any good?' asked Bilbo . . . 'I found it on the ground where the trolls had their fight.' He held out a largish key" (p. 52). In outwitting the trolls, making them fight until the petrifying dawn, Gandalf had deprived them of their key; Bilbo now falls heir to this symbolic tool. Entering the cave, he earns the next important symbol of his manhood; finding "several swords of various makes, shapes, and sizes," Bilbo chooses one of appropriate length, "a knife in a leather sheath," a weapon "as good as a short sword for the hobbit" (pp. 52–53).

Episodes of this sort, and with the same symbolic implications, form the core of the action of the rest of the book: Bilbo the burglar must enter the trolls' cave, the cave under the Misty Mountains, the forgotten tunnel leading to Gollum, Mirkwood, the Elvenking's prison, the lonely mountain, Thorin's cave, and finally his own home (guarded by his harpy cousins, the Sackville-Bagginses), bringing out, respectively, his sword, the Ring, the spiders' dwarf-prisoners, the Elvenking's dwarf-prisoners, Smaug's cup, the Arkenstone, and a place to live.

We must now pull back and attempt to grasp the symbolic implications of Bilbo's history to this point, and perhaps the best way to do so is with the help of Erich Neumann's analysis of the psychological meanings of mythology in his great work *The Origins and History of Consciousness.* I suggested at the beginning that the stories of Bilbo and Frodo are, when examined, Freudian, but it seems clear to me that Freud's analyses of such psychic components as the Oedipus complex do not go nearly so far toward explaining the mythological expressions of this and other universal themes as do the analyses of archetypes provided by Jung, especially as they are refined and extended by Neumann. At any rate, Neumann's work stands as the basis of what follows.

Bilbo's "birth" from Bag End may seem at first puzzling and unnecessary; after all, his natural mother had already borne him once. But "Jung has demonstrated," says Neumann, that basic to the hero's story is his "rebirth, that only as one twice-born is he the hero, and that conversely anyone who has suffered the double birth must be regarded as a hero."[1] Among primitives, ritual allows the young to enter the society of adult males in this way: "rebirth is the sole object of the initiation rites," says Neumann (p. 148), which often involve masked figures of terror who threaten to kill the initiate. "Fire and other symbols of wakefulness and alertness play an important part in the rites of initiation . . . Keeping awake and the endurance of fear, hunger and pain go together as essential elements" of the rituals so that the youth becomes learned in "fortifying the ego and schooling the will" (p. 143). Basic to the completion of the initiation is the attainment of a totemic object; henceforward, the youth "and the totem belong together" (p. 146), it serving as symbol of his maturity. In this context Bilbo's first adventure after leaving Hobbiton, his encounter with the trolls, is clearly his rite of initiation. Sent forward hungry and in the dark toward a mysterious fire, threatened with butchery, injured in a minor way by terrifying figures, forced to lie awake all night in brambly bushes, and finally finding his key and sword, Bilbo takes the first steps toward the maturity needed to meet the dragon. For as Neumann says, "establishing his masculinity [is] the first stage of [the hero's] emancipation" from the womb of helpless infancy. The "successful masculinization of the ego finds expression in its combativeness and readiness to expose itself to the danger which the dragon symbolizes." For Neumann, dragon combat is the ultimate goal of the mythological hero, but the combat often takes symbolic form: "struggle with the dragon is variously represented as the entry into the cave, the descent to the underworld,. . . [an action] frequently taking the form of actual entry into [the mother/womb symbol]" (pp. 152, 154). Bilbo's successive entries into caves or guarded secret places form a series of advancing initiations, gradually preparing him for his final goal, Smaug. For Neumann, "The mythological goal of the dragon fight is almost always the virgin, the captive, or more generally, the 'treasure hard to attain,' " the gaining of which marks the hero's successful emancipation and masculinization (p. 195). Neumann finds that "In the earliest mythologies . . . as well as in fairy tales, legend and poetry, gold and precious stones, but particularly diamonds and pearls . . . miracle rings and wishing rings, magic hoods and winged cloaks, are all symbols of the treasure" (p. 195).

We are now ready to grasp the symbolic implications of Bilbo's adventures, those enterings and graspings listed above. There is no need here to examine all these episodes in detail, since all have essentially the same symbolic thrust. We shall do best to look closely at two key episodes, the events from which all the rest of *The Hobbit* and the *Rings* flows: Bilbo's discoveries of the Ring and the Arkenstone — his "miracle ring" and his diamond.

After leaving Elrond's house at Rivendell, Bilbo and his companions must pass eastward across the Misty Mountains. Seeking shelter from a storm in what appears to be an unused cave, they all fall into an exhausted sleep except Bilbo, who is troubled by nightmares about a "crack in the wall at the back of the cave [that] got bigger and bigger." He awakens to find his dream true, and the opening crack suddenly exudes "big goblins, great ugly-looking goblins" (p. 70), who capture the travelers and haul them back into the womb of the great mountain. Bilbo thus enters a clearly vaginal tunnel guarded by figures of terror — the initial step in the central episodic pattern of *The Hobbit*. Carried before the Great Goblin, and on the verge of execution for possessing Orcrist, the Goblin-cleaver, the hobbit and his companions are suddenly rescued by Gandalf, who kills the King and leads the company to "the very mountain's heart" (p. 76), the dwarves taking turns carrying the smaller and slower Bilbo. But "suddenly Dori, now at the back again carrying Bilbo, was grabbed from behind in the dark. He shouted and fell; and the hobbit rolled off his shoulders into the blackness, bumped his head on hard rock, and remembered nothing more" (p. 78).

Bilbo awakens to find himself lost and alone, frightened and unsure of himself — this time in the dark, wet depths of the Misty Mountains — and, symbolically, just as he was in the beginning, alone in a "womb," unknowing of all that goes on outside (he is now separated from Gandalf and the dwarves and does not know where they are). Initially he had had the Wise Old Man to shove him out of his hobbit-hole (minus pocket handkerchief, to be sure) and into the wide world. But he has now advanced beyond that original sexless and helpless embryonic state, for he possesses his as yet untried sword, his yet unused phallic extension; he has grown, but only slightly, and will begin the next stage of his initiation accidentally, lost and groping:

> His head was swimming, and he was far from certain even of the direction they had been going in when he had his fall. He guessed as well as he could, and crawled along for a good way, till suddenly his hand met what felt like a tiny ring of cold metal lying on the floor of the tunnel. It was a turning point in his career, but he did not know it. He put the ring in his pocket almost without thinking; certainly it did not seem of any particular use at the moment. He did not go much further, but sat down on the cold floor and gave himself up to complete miserableness (p. 79).

As we might expect of Bilbo in such a plight, he momentarily regresses, trying to pop his thumb into his mouth, as it were: "After some time he felt for his pipe. It was not broken, and that was something. Then he felt for his pouch, and there was some tobacco in it, and that was something more. Then he felt for matches and he could not find any at all, and that shattered his hopes completely" (p. 80). Feeling about for his matches, however, Bilbo finds an object inside his pants for which he has yet discovered no use, but something far more valuable than a thumb; for Bilbo is not in his Bag-womb anymore, where a thumb would be useful. He is now in the depths where the hero must descend to find the treasure and deploy his sword. He has already found the treasure, and now, "in slapping all his pockets and feeling all round himself for matches his hand came on the hilt of his little sword — the little dagger that he got from the trolls, and that he had quite forgotten; . . . he wore it inside his breeches" (p. 80). Inside his breeches indeed! And where else?

Having recalled to mind his totem of manliness, having forgotten his regressive desire for a pipe, and most importantly having found his first symbol of the "treasure hard to attain," the ring of invisibility (though he doesn't know *that* yet), Bilbo is ready to face Gollum. His encounter with this voracious and wicked creature is in fact Bilbo's chief preparation for his major encounter with Smaug. These two episodes are closely parallel, both involving riddles and invisibility, both ending with Bilbo's narrow escape from the perilous tunnel of the treasure's wicked guard. In each episode, Bilbo descends, trades riddles, and outwits the terror or grasps his weakness (Gollum cannot guess what is in Bilbo's pocket and cannot see him invisible; Smaug does not know he has revealed the bare patch in his breast). Then the hobbit flees invisibly and narrowly escapes, but loses something in the process (his buttons, the hair of his head and heels). The first episode, however, is more childlike and "fun," at least in its inspiration; Bilbo's button-loss reminds one of Peter Rabbit's loss as he flees from Mr. McGregor's cabbage patch, while the second encounter is more perilous, closer to *Beowulf* than to "Peter Rabbit" (Bilbo steals a cup from Smaug on his first visit to the dragon's chamber, even as did the nameless servant in the ancient epic). The chief difference between the two scenes is, of course, inside Bilbo himself. In the first, he is immature and timid, in the second he is mature and courageous; the one, clearly, is preparation for the other: he must find the ring before he can use it.

By the time Bilbo and the dwarves reach the Lonely Mountain, the hobbit has "more [spirit] than the others" (p. 218) and is in fact "the real leader in their adventure" (p. 233). And once again, the finding and entering of the tunnel in the side of the mountain reads like a Freudian test case. On the west side of the Lonely Mountain, two spurs of what appear on Thror's Map (p. 6) to be giant talus slopes thrust outward like two great legs. Bilbo and the dwarves enter the valley between the legs and ascend the mountain searching for the door. True to form, it is Bilbo who finds it, and, as usual, the description of the secret entrance reverberates with psychosexual overtones: "a little steep-walled bay, grassy-floored, still and quiet. Its entrance ... looked like a dark crack" (p. 219). Again it is Bilbo who signals the proper time to use the key to enter that opening, just as "a red ray of the sun escaped like a finger through a rent in the cloud," and a "gleam of light came straight through the opening," illuminating the keyhole: "A hole appeared suddenly about three feet from the ground ... 'The key! The key!' cried Bilbo" (p. 223).

On his first secret visit to Smaug's chamber, Bilbo takes a large two-handled cup in order to impress Thorin and his fellows ("I've done it! This will show them. 'More like a grocer than a burglar' indeed!" [p. 228]) — an act modeled directly after Tolkien's source, section 32 of *Beowulf*, where the slave at odds with his master steals a precious plated cup from the worm of that tale in order to placate his angry lord. Aside from the authority of the source, however, a cup is an ideal symbolic object for the hero to grasp from the dragon, because as one critic of romance has noted, "cups and hollow vessels [have, as quest objects,] female sexual affinities." [2]

I have attempted this "mythic" approach to *The Hobbit* not because it tells all there is to know about the book but because it tells something important about the nature of Tolkien's vision and the world he created that could perhaps not be told in another way. *The Hobbit* can be read consistently from this angle because it is a book written out of profound imaginative depths, right from the deep of the mythic imagination. The story Tolkien has to tell — a story about being born into a world of heroic necessities and having continually to descend into the dark depths of experience to confront the black elements of one's own self and the world and there to conquer them — shapes itself into the same pattern of experience undergone by every hero who has walked the storied earth. This pattern, to use another brand of jargon, is "archetypal" and has been described by Joseph Campbell in this way:

> The mythological hero, setting forth from his commonday hut or castle, is lured, carried away, or else voluntarily proceeds, to the threshold of adventure. There he encounters a shadow presence that guards the passage. The hero may defeat or conciliate this power and go alive into the kingdom of the dark (brother-battle, dragon-battle . . .), or be slain by the opponent and descend in death (dismemberment, crucifixion). Beyond the threshold, then, the hero journeys through a world of unfamiliar yet strangely intimate forces, some of which severely threaten him (tests), some of which give magical aid (helpers). When he arrives at the nadir of the mythological round, he undergoes a supreme ordeal

and gains his reward. The triumph may be represented as the hero's sexual union with the goddess-
mother of the world (sacred marriage), his recognition by the father-creator (father atonement), or
again — if the powers have remained unfriendly to
him — his theft of the boon he came to gain (bride-
theft, fire-theft); intrinsically it is an expansion of
consciousness and therewith of being (illumination,
transfiguration, freedom). The final work is that of
the return. If the powers have blessed the hero,
he now sets forth under their protection (emissary);
if not, he flees and is pursued (transformation flight,
obstacle flight). At the return threshold the tran-
scendental powers must remain behind; the hero
re-emerges from the kingdom of dread (return,
resurrection). The boon that he brings restores the
world.[3]

Tolkien discovered and worked out this pattern of experience
in the creation of *The Hobbit*, finding in the process that it
was the one theme that really mattered to him as storyteller.
His real discovery is, of course, not the theme of the hero —
that is ancient indeed — his real discovery is the thrilling
potential of the mythic imagination, that it can tell us things
about ourselves and our world we may not know in another
way, things we need deeply.

The perceptive reader will have guessed by now that much
of this chapter is a parody of what William Empson did
for (or should I say *to?*) *Alice in Wonderland*[4] rather than a
fully serious criticism. Yet there is a point in what I have
done, though it is only the beginning of a real explanation
of *The Hobbit*. Taken in and for itself, Tolkien's children's
story deserves little serious, purely literary criticism. But we

cannot take *The Hobbit* by itself, for it stands at the threshold of one of the most immense and satisfying imaginative creations of our time, *The Lord of the Rings*. The real importance of *The Hobbit* is what its creator learned in the writing. As Bilbo Baggins grew up, so did Tolkien's imagination. The childlike evocations of shivery evil in Bilbo's adventures awoke in Tolkien a sudden and disturbing perception of genuine evil and of the heroism it must elicit. So we have to begin again with *The Hobbit*, seeing it in the perspective it deserves, as an initiation (both Tolkien's and Bilbo's) into the perilous world of Faërie, a world Tolkien only slowly discovered and only with much labor gave, in turn, to us.

Tolkien learned so much in writing *The Hobbit* he had to do the whole thing again, differently. The children's story is an experiment in form, delightful for what it is, but curiously structured. As should be clear from what Neumann has said about the hero, the two central scenes in *The Hobbit*, if it is to be a story about a hero who faces a dragon and attains a treasure, ought to be Bilbo's encounter with Gollum after he has found the Ring and his encounter with Smaug just before he finds the Arkenstone. But as I have shown, Tolkien's conception of what he was doing in *The Hobbit* developed far beyond its original treasure-grasping motif even as he wrote — a development that caused a curious lack of structural coherence in his children's book. For if *The Hobbit* were to keep within the traditional structure of the quest fairy tale, the story ought to have a minor climax in the encounter with Gollum and the Ring (Bilbo thus finding a magical way to face Smaug invisibly) and a major climax in the encounter with the dragon and the attainment of the Arkenstone. Bilbo ought then to take his treasure home and live happily ever after. But of course the book does not end that way at all. The real climax of *The Hobbit* is not Bilbo's *finding* the Arkenstone, but his *renouncing* the Arkenstone. But we are not, even with this insight, at the real structural center of the narrative of Bilbo, for in the larger context of the story of the One Ring, not even *this* episode is the heart of Bilbo's career. For what in fact, in its own context, ought to be the *minor* climax of Bilbo's story (his discovery of the Ring) is, from the perspective of *The Lord of the Rings*, the most important moment in the book, the beginning of the whole vast tale of Middle-earth. When we grasp the nature of this unexpected climax and its importance to Tolkien's imagination, we have come close to understanding the reason why he had to retell the plot husk of *The Hobbit* in a larger sequel. The children's book began as a symmetrical quest-tale ("There and Back Again," its subtitle) about entering, grasping, and returning, but it grew into a story not about grasping but about renouncing, and thus in its own context turned out to be an asymmetrical plot. When, however, we place the end of *The Hobbit* up against the beginning of *The Lord of the Rings*, we indeed find a structural symmetry: a symmetry of renunciation. Bilbo gives up the Ring at the beginning of *The Fellowship of the Ring*, even as he gave up the Arkenstone at the end of *The Hobbit*. Bilbo's story demanded *The Lord of the Rings*; its asymmetry cried out for balance. And Tolkien was not slow to heed the call.

Having discovered his pattern and his theme in *The Hobbit*, and their great potentials, Tolkien set about telling the same story again in *The Lord of the Rings*, yet with a difference. For though Frodo, too, as I have shown, has a sequence of adventures closely parallel to Bilbo's, the sequence in the *Rings* of entering a forbidden place and taking forth a symbol of manhood does not exhaust the adventures of the Ringbearer; he has more to do. Frodo's "tunnel" or "forbidden valley" adventures, in which he faces a terrifying creature and from which he takes a valuable object or new knowledge essential to the quest, comprise only *part* of his task: he must, threatened by the Black Riders, enter the valley of the Withywindle to face Old Man Willow, taking thence the knowledge, supplied by Tom Bombadil, of the ways and wiles of the Old Forest; he must enter the barrow to face the Wight, rescue his friends, and earn his sword; he must enter the mines under the Misty Mountains, there to strike the foot of the Cave Troll; he must face Shelob in her cave; and, finally, he must ascend Mount Doom, enter its tunnel, and undergo his final test of will. But these are only *some* of his tests. In other words, *The Lord of the Rings* is not exclusively in the initiatory mode of *The Hobbit*, is not, that is, merely a book addressed to children, symbolically expressing their fears and wishes about growing up. *The Hobbit* is pure myth of maturation, with no other overlay of "meaning." *The Lord of the Rings,* however, despite Tolkien's demurrer that it has no "inner meaning or 'message' " (I, p. 6), has a definite mythic argument and a positive moral and aesthetic, even a "political" program. In his children's story, Tolkien does little more than bore down to the artesian archetype and let it flow. But the more it flowed, the more he recognized the potential greatness of his theme and that the mythic devices he had rediscovered could, rightly used, be a searching and a healing tool. So in a generation that had forgotten the power and value of myth, he set about creating a group of myths of central concern to our age. The next chapter is a discussion of these larger implications in *The Lord of the Rings.*

FRODO ANTI-FAUST

The Lord of the Rings *as*
Contemporary Mythology

The two great external facts of our time are the explosion
of populations and the explosions of the new energies.
The two great internal facts of our time are the re-creation
of the devil (or pure behavior) in a place of authority and
the development of techniques for finding destructive
troubles in the psyche of individuals.

— R. P. BLACKMUR

By dipping them in myth we see them more clearly.

— C. S. LEWIS

WHY DO certain contemporary readers seem to require
so absolutely what Tolkien has to give to the extent
that regularly, on completion of the third volume of *The Lord
of the Rings,* they begin again on the first? Perhaps the outlines
of an answer emerge from a remark by Stanley Hyman in
The Tangled Bank, his study of the four chief myth-breakers
of our time, Darwin, Marx, Frazer, and Freud. Hyman
compares T. K. Cheynes's monumental *Encyclopedia Biblica*
of 1903 with the *Oxford Dictionary of the Christian Church,*
published in 1957. The first, he says, with its triumphantly
reasonable conclusions about the human origins and
wayward evolution of the biblical text, seems not so much

the beginning of something completed in our own time as a "splendid monument to the nineteenth century's frustrated hopes for the rational intelligence." The second, on the other hand, once again securely neoorthodox after a half century of painful struggle, seems as something from a "thousand years earlier," a sign that "all that a century of labor had painfully uncovered is once more buried under the sea of faith."[1] Indeed it ought to be clear by now that our century has been not so much an age of demythologizing as of remythologizing, a time of agonized and sometimes frenzied search for new mythologies, new explanations for an increasingly incomprehensible world.

Hyman has put his finger on a real epistemological sore spot. We know, we modern rationalists, that myth contains no real "knowledge" (at least as we now define the term), yet when we deflate and discard myth, we find gaping windy holes in our defenses against the cold terrors of pain and death. The problem is already an old one. The nineteenth century, and much of our own, troubled and put on the defensive by the myth-destructive forces unleashed by such thinkers as Darwin and Freud, began to lose faith in any kind of mythologizing. The greatest capitulation (or victory) came when religious thinkers began to assert that religion and myth were things apart, that myth-making was not, essentially, a sacral activity. William Blake was probably the first great English thinker to foresee the disastrous consequences of such an idea for the literary imagination and the soul's health and set about, perhaps even before he was needed, attacking it with the profound force of such polemics as "What is a Church & what is a Theatre, Are they two and not one?" and "Jesus & his Apostles & Disciples were all Artists."[2] Indeed perhaps one of the reasons the English-reading world started needing Blake (more than fifty years after his death) was that he spoke to this very issue, asserting the sacral functions of the artistic, mythopoeic imagination and giving answers that people like Yeats needed desperately.[3]

At any rate it seems to me that Tolkien speaks to this issue for the second half of our century, reasserting the supreme importance of the myth-making imagination and providing, in the process, a set of myths that express, more fully than the works of any other contemporary writer I know, a complex of otherwise inexpressible emotions riving the breasts of a whole generation of readers. The feelings I speak of are the emotional correlatives of the cultural "facts" so aptly described by R. P. Blackmur at the head of this chapter; the myths preside over our response to *The Lord of the Rings.*

The need to be, if only for brief moments, in a world of coherence, where all is relevant and has meaning, is a profoundly human need and one that was for most of our culture's history satisfied by religious myths. During that time a cosmos was given shape, significance, and destiny by its Christian foundations. That world, for many, no longer exists, but when it did art spoke with a greater resonance, being couched in stories and symbols rich in context and interrelationship. It is of course now a commonplace of criticism that the modern artist must create his own cosmos of mythical significances before he can set his creatures afoot in it, must devise a symbolism before its resonances may sound. Tolkien, for our time, has created such a world with his Middle-earth, and the actions transpiring in that world have symbolic relevance to some of the profoundest issues of our age, specifically, we might say, to those cultural facts named by Blackmur.

The most striking of Blackmur's facts is what he calls the "explosions of the new energies," a fact of such consequence for the postwar imagination that immense emotional energies must be expended continuously by our psyches just to keep us from going insane in the face of it. Like it or not, we all subliminally contemplate the Bomb, waking and dreaming, and are all in need of useful ways to pattern and express the destructive emotions evoked by this fact. Now Tolkien, like Blake, knew well that the literary imagination is perhaps our richest source of mythological expressions of internal states. Literature gives us ways of looking at our situation that are unavailable elsewhere: ways of taking it apart and reassembling it to make sense and ways of coming to terms with it emotionally. In *The Lord of the Rings*, Tolkien has symbolically expressed our situation in a strikingly profound and useful set of myths that can evoke and pattern a healing emotional response to literary situations deeply symbolic of our own. We must carefully note that the *Rings* patterns a response to its *own* situation, not directly to ours. Literature gives no direct moral answers, it only exercises and enriches the wisdom of spirit that must ponder and respond to its own dilemmas. Tolkien himself has seen the possibilities for finding simple-minded allegory in his work and has repeatedly insisted that the Ring is not the atom bomb and the War of the Rings is not World War II. We need not doubt his sincerity; a powerful symbol is not the allegorical equivalent of a single technological item. The Ring does not equal the Bomb, but is rather a symbol for the entire complex fact that twentieth-century man has, like Frodo, suddenly found himself, without wanting it, without even guessing it would find a way into his pocket, in possession of a power over nature so immense even the desire to use it will inevitably corrupt his soul. And again, like Frodo, he would really rather throw the whole thing into the sea and forget it, but knows he cannot. Here we arrive at a perception of one of Tolkien's supremely valuable contributions to the imaginative health of us all — what I have called the anti-Faustian myth.

From the end of the Middle Ages to the first nuclear explosion (to be overly precise) our deepest spiritual urges have been Faustian, directing our emotional and intellectual energies in an endless quest for knowledge of and power over nature, over our world. Now we have become like Sauron; we *can* control nature, but we find in the process that every controlling touch spoils and corrupts. Like Sauron, we can darken the sky, blast the vegetation, pervert and control even the minds of men; and again like Sauron, we remain the prisoners of our own assumptions, seeing no alternative to ever expanding our corrupting control. It is gradually becoming apparent, however, that a different course is necessary if humankind is to survive, and some of the finer spirits among us are suggesting that course, Tolkien not least among them: simplify, put away the desire to control and thereby pervert nature, resubmit to the pattern of nature's rhythms. Those who so argue place themselves in Frodo's position, or, to put it another way, the hobbits are Tolkien's symbols for this anti-Faustian urge. Frodo has the Ring, the symbol of all corrupting power, and his every desire is to *get rid of it*. Even at the risk of letting it fall again into the blackened hand of Sauron, he must try to destroy this source and symbol of the Faustian will to power and knowledge so that he may return in peace to Tolkien's Great Good Place, the Shire, the quiet little land ruled only by the swing of the seasons.

Blackmur's internal cultural facts also receive mythic treatment in *The Lord of the Rings*. Tolkien is indeed a keen analyst
of the modern psyche and its need for realignment with the
natural world; he was one of the first to grasp that everything
depends on whether we can adjust our ego-ideals away from
the Faustian and toward whatever it is Frodo represents — Frodo anti-Faust but by no means Frodo anti-hero.
Frodo is hero, but surely that word must undergo some radical
changes in meaning to be applicable to a three-foot-high
bundle of timidity with furry feet. This indeed is another
of Tolkien's gifts to us in *The Lord of the Rings* — a profound
criticism and revaluation of the meaning of heroic behavior.
He did not, however, summon the insight overnight but rather
developed it over a period of years as his own vision of
his world and its meanings grew. Perhaps the clearest picture
of Tolkien's deepening notions about the nature of heroic
behavior can be found in a comparison of his lecture on
Beowulf before the British Academy in 1936 with his brief
essay on *The Battle of Maldon* published in *Essays and Studies*
for 1953, dates important in the history of Tolkien's world,
as the first is the year *The Lord of the Rings* was begun, and
the second is the year before its initial two volumes were
published. The two works present strikingly different attitudes toward heroism, and as is usual with Tolkien, his critical
thinking is a function of his creative interests at the time.
As chapter I has shown, the *Beowulf* lecture was to a
considerable extent the outgrowth of Tolkien's creative strug-
gles with *The Hobbit* and its mythological depiction of radical
evil in a literary universe. He argued that in the heroic
literature of northern Europe, and in *Beowulf* pre-eminently,
the mythical sense of radical evil expresses itself in the form
of monsters like Grendel and the Worm. The glory of that

literature, he declared, is that it recognizes and does not shirk the question of radical evil, potent beyond man's measure to conquer, nor does it flinch in the face of inevitable defeat, but — and this is its greatness — poises a hero in foredoomed but magnificent conflict, seeking the only death with meaning in a pre-Christian world — bravely fighting the unconquerable. Tolkien was perhaps the first critic of *Beowulf* to express forthrightly the metaphysical stance darkly stated in the mythology of the poem — a despair that yet cast a cold eye on death, giving it the dignity of Beowulf's own defeat.

Finding historical parallels to moments of critical insight is dangerous but always fascinating; in this case, it was but four years after Tolkien expressed the spirit of Beowulf's heroism that it reappeared in the eye and voice of Winston Churchill, and thence the nation, during the Battle of Britain. The parallel need be taken as no more than a curiosity, yet surely one of the central tasks of criticism is to find, and when necessary rediscover, in the literature of a nation, the spirit and will of whatever kind of heroic endeavor it may need. This fruitful collaboration between literature and criticism can be doubly rich if the heroic author is critic as well, for what the writer needs in order to create is likewise what the critic (as representative, intellect, as it were, of his society) needs in order to see clearly. In 1936 Tolkien needed a clear grasp of the mythological revelation of the workings of radical evil and of the heroic necessities evil creates. Writing *The Hobbit* gave him that clear grasp, and, as a gift almost, a critical footnote to creative discovery, it taught him also how to read *Beowulf* in a way precisely relevant to England's need at the time for insight into heroic behavior. Then, feeding on what he had learned from writing *The Hobbit* and from reading *Beowulf* through the lenses of Middle-earth,

Tolkien gave us *The Lord of the Rings*; and behold, another gift: he had learned yet another new insight into *Beowulf* and a new way to read *The Battle of Maldon*, finding once again a critique and evaluation of heroic behavior deeply relevant to the changed needs of his society. For what England needed in 1940 was much different from what she, and the world, needed in 1953. Too neatly put, the reason for the difference was the war and all its aftermath, specifically the need for what I have defined as an anti-Faustian myth. It would be too much to say that Tolkien changed his view of heroic behavior because of World War II; indeed he has made plain that the First War affected him far more deeply than the Second. His mind and views changed during his sojourn in Middle-earth, facing Sauron with Frodo and Sam, not facing Hitler with his countrymen. But the internal experience of the best writers is the internal history of their age, and no less is true of Tolkien. He saw in 1953 that part of Beowulf's heroism was pointless bravado, excess "chivalry": Beowulf in facing Grendel without a sword, and the Worm with only a sword, was doing little more than show off. Tolkien's perception in 1953 is that "this 'northern heroic spirit' [which in 1936 he had tried to make the British Academy understand was indissolubly tied to a living mythology] is never quite pure; it is of gold and an alloy. Unalloyed it would direct a man to endure even death unflinching, when necessary: that is when death may help the achievement of some object of will, or when life can only be purchased by denial of what one stands for. But since such conduct is held admirable, the alloy of personal good name was never wholly absent." So Beowulf seems not so admirable in 1953 as he did in 1936. Even in his fight with Grendel, Beowulf "does more than he need, eschewing weapons in order to make his struggle . . . a 'sporting' fight: which will enhance his personal glory, though it will put him in unnecessary peril, and weaken his chances of ridding the Danes of an intolerable affliction" (*Essays and Studies*, p. 14). His action is saved from being altogether reprehensible by the twin facts that he wins (victory covers a multitude of sins) and that he acts as an independent agent, with "no responsibilities downwards" (*Essays and Studies*, p. 15) for the lives of others. He has not this excuse, however, when he battles the Worm; as king of the Geats "he does not rid himself of his chivalry, the excess persists, even when he is an old king upon whom all the hopes of a people rest" (*Essays and Studies*, p. 15). Beowulf's responsibility is clear; he must seek not his own glory but the welfare of his people, and in this he fails: "He will not deign to lead a force against the dragon, as wisdom might direct even a hero to do; for, as he explains in a long 'vaunt', his many victories have relieved him of fear" (*Essays and Studies*, p. 15). But apparently they have not taught him the duties of a king:

> He is saved from defeat, and the essential object, destruction of the dragon, only achieved by the loyalty of a subordinate. Beowulf's chivalry would otherwise have ended in his own useless death, with the dragon still at large. As it is, a subordinate is placed in greater peril than he need have been, and though he does not pay the penalty of his master's *mod* [pride] with his own life, the people lose their king disastrously (*Essays and Studies*, pp. 15–16).

Tolkien's new insight into *Beowulf*, altogether different from what he needed to see (and had been taught to see by *The Hobbit*) in 1936, is coupled with enriched insight into another heroic poem, *The Battle of Maldon.* He settles upon, and retranslates, two lines in the poem the significance of which suddenly looms up, in our own time and in the light of Frodo's and Sam's experiences in Mordor, in a way it could not have done in 1936: *ða se eorl ongan for his ofermode alyfan landes to fela laþere ðeode* ("then the earl in his overmastering pride actually yielded ground to the enemy, as he should not have done"). Tolkien finds, in 1953, that the more standard translation of W. P. Ker does not fully express the poem's intended criticism of Beorhtnoth's prideful excess, his "sporting" act of letting the Vikings freely cross the causeway to better fighting position: "then the earl of his overboldness granted ground too much to the hateful people" (*Essays and Studies,* p. 16). Unlike Ker, Tolkien sees severe criticism of the earl in the line, for his making a " 'sporting fight' on level terms" with the enemy took place at "other people's expense. In his situation he was not a subordinate, but the authority to be obeyed on the spot; and he was responsible for all the men under him, not to throw away their lives except with one object, the defence of the realm from an implacable foe" (*Essays and Studies,* p. 15). The true heroism in this situation was not the *ofermod* ("overmastering pride") of Beorhtnoth but the endurance of his men, forced by his prideful act to exhibit their loyalty to the death. For, as Tolkien concluded in 1953, it "is the heroism of obedience and love not of pride or willfulness that is the most heroic and most moving; from Wiglaf under his kinsman's shield, to Beorhtwold at Maldon, down to Balaclava," and, Tolkien might as well have added, down to Sam at Orodruin. If we look closely here, we shall once again find Tolkien's professional scholarship following upon, even standing as implicit commentary upon his own creative work of the time.

Moreover, the scholarly revaluation and critique of the heroic poem is printed only a few months before the work for which it is a covert preparation — *The Lord of the Rings*. The little essay on *The Battle of Maldon* is the critical fruit of Middle-earthly discovery and the preparation of an audience for the new mode of heroism he has formulated through Frodo and Sam, even as the *Beowulf* essay was preparation for *The Hobbit*. And again, this new mode of heroism (renunciation of power for the sake of all men) is precisely relevant to the changed needs of the world to which *The Lord of the Rings* addresses itself, for the world had the Bomb in 1953, as it did not in 1940: it no longer needed the bravado and recklessness of a Beowulf or the *ofermod* of a Beorhtnoth, but as never before required restraint, national as well as personal selflessness, and a concern for the good of all rather than merely of the national group. It required, in other words, precisely the human equivalent of the self-effacing hobbit heroism of Frodo and Sam, death to the contemporary equivalents of Boromir, and, most of all, an end to the desires of Sauron.

Mention of Tolkien's spirit of malice, Sauron, brings us to another of Blackmur's internal cultural facts, the re-creation of the devil in our own age. Tolkien's personification of the urge toward power is in fact a Middle-earthly version of Satan; even his name smacks of serpent-ness, probably coming from the Greek *sauros*, "lizard." We know already of Tolkien's strong feelings about the imaginative value and literary propriety of mythological representations of radical evil; for him, myth is one of our most perfect and least valued ways of fully perceiving the real, and in this, of course, he has the tradition of Western culture behind him. The myth of a personal Satan provided for centuries a satisfactory resting place for our notions of evil and its workings and an at least sometimes healthy source of enriching imaginative activity (*Paradise Lost*, for example). The gradual death of that myth, along with many others, has left a large hole in our imaginative grasp of reality; we lack working imaginative constructs to do justice to our real sense that there is radical or at least inexplicable evil in our experience. It seems not unreasonable that imaginative poverty in this regard would result in the inability to see the world clearly. An inadequate imaginative apprehension of evil, worse yet, could result in the inability to understand our experience and in the casual acceptance of barely perceived evil. The gassing of Jews can easily be screened behind abstractions like "the final solution," the burning of Vietnamese villages explained away with empty jargon like "pacification" if the imagination is too weak to conjure a living sympathy for what is actually happening.

I think a sizable part of our culture has long since felt the pang of imaginative hunger; there is little doubt that much of the history of our century has been the symptom (or cause) of numberless desperate attempts to create or revive mythological systems to explain what has gone wrong. If I read the present climate correctly, part of the reason Tolkien's vision is so necessary to so many is that it provides a richly satisfying experience of a fully worked out mythological perception of radical evil. Tolkien's particular myth parallels his Christianity, positing a malevolent and corrupting outside influence, spiritual and probably eternal, against which man is doomed to fight, but which he has no hope of conquering on his own — Sauron the Great, Lord of the Rings. Sauron's career is modeled after those of the biblical and Miltonic Satan. In Appendix A of *The Return of the King,* Tolkien gives a brief sketch of Sauron's history, and it is clear that he finds the Satan myth an altogether satisfying center for his own exploration of radical evil. Originally Sauron was a fair creature to look upon and had been given supremacy in Middle-earth. The original men, the Númenoreans, had been placed, like Adam, under a single prohibition, not to set foot upon the Undying Lands to the west; the command was called the Ban of the Valar. Toward the end of the Second Age, Sauron bewitched the king of Númenor and most of his subjects, telling them that "everlasting life would be his who possessed the Undying Lands, and that the Ban was imposed only to prevent the Kings of Men from surpassing the Valar." Deceived, the Númenoreans committed Middle-earth's Original Sin, their kingdom was destroyed, and Sauron fell with them. The "bodily form in which he long had walked perished; but he fled back to Middle-earth, a spirit of hatred borne upon a dark wind. He was unable ever again to assume a form that seemed fair to men, but became black and hideous" (III, p. 317). Sauron's story aligns, point by point, with Satan's.

Sauron's imps, the Orcs, are likewise expressions of one of Blackmur's cultural facts, the discovery of techniques for finding destructive troubles in men's psyches. Tolkien is, of course, no psychoanalyst, but his Orcs are the products of a keenly perceptive imaginative grasp of the side of the human mind that has traditionally been associated with energy and evil; they are, in Freudian terminology, id projections, and perhaps the best way to see what Tolkien is doing with these hideous creatures is with the careful application of the kind of analysis Blackmur mentions. To say what the Orcs are, where they come from, and what they are related to is to reveal a fascinating aspect of Tolkien's mythological imagination.

Tolkien the philologist probably took his word "Orc" from *Orcus*, the Italic god of death and the underworld and the original of the French word *ogre*. And by a remarkable coincidence, if it is one, Tolkien's name for the foulest imaginable picture of humanity is the same as William Blake's name for the fairest picture, his revolutionary figure Orc. Where Blake got his word is still in debate. S. Foster Damon suggests that the word is an anagram of the Latin *cor*, "heart"[4]; the *Oxford English Dictionary* tells us that as early as 1611 "orc," from the Latin *orca*, "whale," denoted in English a devouring land or sea monster, and Harold Bloom has suggested that Blake knew enough Latin to derive "Orc" from the same *Orcus* Tolkien quite independently drew upon.[5] I am not so much interested in the names, however, as in what a comparison of Blake's and Tolkien's attitudes toward and literary uses of their creatures can tell us about the vision of life in Tolkien's mythic argument.

Both Orcs are symbols or representatives of a disruptive power inimical to established order, whose function is to rebel against and overthrow the status quo. But from this point, the parallel between the two Orcs becomes a polarity, for whereas in the radical Blakean vision the status quo is destructive and sterile, in Tolkien the status quo of the Shire is the thing most desirable. In Blake, Orc appears as a symbolic picture of the return of the repressed to the level of consciousness by the vehicle of political revolution; he is the inevitable result of sexual repression, which Blake, unlike Freud, regarded as inimical rather than necessary to civilized life. Though disagreeing with Freud about the necessity of repression, Blake anticipated by more than a hundred years the psychoanalytic insight that the energies of the id, when denied outlet in one form, will find an exit in another form, often with terrible psychic or physical violence. In the terms of Blake's myth, when the psychological category he calls Luvah (probably derived from the word "love" and loosely identifiable with the id) is repressed (in the myth, chained down by the father-figure Urthona — "Earth-owner?"), it will break forth with terrible force as Orc, the "vehicular form" of Luvah or the aspect of Luvah perceivable in the world of time and space, as political revolution.

In Blake's myth, the sexual nature of this terrible force is glorified and given powerful mythic statement in the Preludium to *America: A Prophecy.* Here, the American Revolution, or rather the mythic figure of revolution itself, appears as a saving explosion of long-repressed libidinal energy. "Red Orc" has been chained in an underworld (a "dark abode") by his repressive father Urthona for fourteen years, or until he has reached sexual maturity, at which point the chains of repression can hold him no longer:

> Silent as despairing love, and strong as jealousy,
> The hairy shoulders rend the links; free are the wrists of fire.

Once released from the iron links of repression, Orc's first act is sexual: he copulates with his sister and keeper, the "shadowy Daughter of Urthona":

> Round the terrific loins he seiz'd the panting, struggling womb:
> It joy'd: she put aside her clouds & smil'd her first-born smile.
>
> (*America,* Plate 2)

In Blake, then, political revolution revitalizes, indeed impregnates; political violence is overtly sexualized.

The Lord of the Rings can likewise be seen as a political fantasy expressed in covert sexual symbols. Its basic subject is the end of one world order — the Third Age of Middleearth — and the competition between the two world orders seeking to replace it; the Fourth Age will be either that of Sauron and the Orcs or that of man. As it turns out, Sauron loses, whereas in Blake, Orc wins. This is very instructive and tells us much about the contrast between the two authors. For though the perspectives and sympathies toward the two Orcs are radically different, their underworlds and their figures are presented in the same kind of infernal and sexual imagery. Just as Orc's "dark abode" is in "regions of dark death" and "black cloud," deep in "caverns" of the earth (*America*, Plate 1), so is Mordor a hell of ashes and smoke. As Frodo and Sam stand ready to enter Sauron's infernal land, they see Mount Doom,

> its feet founded in ashen ruin, its huge cone rising to a great height, where its reeking head was swathed in cloud. Its fires were now dimmed, and it stood in smouldering slumber, as threatening and dangerous as a sleeping beast. Behind it there hung a vast shadow . . .
>
> Frodo and Sam gazed out in mingled loathing and wonder on this hateful land. Between them and the smoking mountain . . . all seemed ruinous and dead, a desert burned and choked (III, p. 200).

And just as Orc's nature is purely libidinous, as is clear from his first act of freedom, so the Orcs are rabbit-like in their breeding and swarming. Sauron has spawned literally millions of them in his desire for armies, and Saruman has even gone so far as to crossbreed men and Orcs to form the hideous Uruk-hai. Again, the two creatures are almost preternaturally alike in the symbolic character of their appearance, though their actual physical likenesses are worlds apart. Just as Orc's most interesting (and only noted) secondary sexual characteristic, his body hair, has been located with symbolic propriety in his place of greatest strength — his "hairy shoulders" that "rend the links" of sexual repression — so Tolkien's Orcs have long hairy arms, the strength of which is terrifying.

The two figures are, that is, mythological expressions of the same psychological category, but are presented from entirely different perspectives; indeed, the authors' descriptions of their creatures reveal, as well as anything else, their views of what their imaginations have summoned. Whereas Orc is a beautiful adolescent boy and quite properly naked, the Orcs have "hideous" faces and "foul breath," are "bowlegged," and wear "long hairy breeches of some unclean beast-fell," the scent of which causes "disgust" in Frodo (II, p. 58; III, pp. 189, 190).

Indeed Tolkien's revulsion from the Orcs is a chief motive force behind *The Lord of the Rings*; they *must* be pushed back into Mordor and held there. Tolkien wants Orc-hood sealed in precisely the same underworld of the mind from which Blake wants it to erupt; the one, that is, accepts the necessity of repression, the other argues that repression in any form is damaging to the soul.

Tolkien's mythological answer to Blackmur's fourth cultural fact, the explosion of populations, will be unacceptable to most moderns, though it is the only one Tolkien's own church can sanction: the orderly sexual restraint of the hobbits. Whereas the Orcs breed rapidly, the hobbits marry

late and do not even count as men until age thirty-three
(I, p. 30). And whereas the Orcs are covered with hair, in part
to represent their sexual voraciousness and animality, the
hobbits' body hair has been displaced downward; their
secondary sexual characteristic is located in the most apt of
symbolic places, the feet (they have no beards).

The hobbits' homeland, the tradition-bound, backward-
looking Shire, is an idealized version of preindustrial England
that clearly grows out of Tolkien's own conservative, nostalgic
view of the land of his youth. He has written:

> Not long ago — incredible though it may seem — I
> heard a clerk of Oxenford declare that he "wel-
> comed" the proximity of mass-production robot
> factories, and the roar of self-obstructive mechanical
> traffic, because it brought his university into "con-
> tact with real life." He may have meant that the
> way men were living and working in the twentieth
> century was increasing in barbarity at an alarming
> rate, and that the loud demonstrations of this in
> the streets of Oxford might serve as a warning that
> it is not possible to preserve for long an oasis of
> sanity in a desert of unreason by mere fences,
> without actual offensive action (practical and intel-
> lectual). I fear he did not . . . The notion that motor-
> cars are more "alive" than, say, centaurs or dragons
> is curious; that they are more "real" than, say, horses
> is pathetically absurd. (TL, p. 62).

In *The Lord of the Rings*, this attitude is dramatized when Frodo
and his companions return to the Shire after the destruction
of the Ring only to find that in their absence Saruman has
industrialized the homeland. Tolkien's description of Hobbiton might have come out of a D. H. Lawrence novel:

The great chimney rose up before them; and as they
drew near the old village across the water, through
rows of new mean houses . . . they saw the new mill
in all its frowning and dirty ugliness: a great brick
building straddling the stream, which it fouled with
a steaming and stinking outflow (III, p. 296).

Here is the point at which the polarity between Blake's
and Tolkien's visions of life begins to turn back into a parallel,
for Blake too was appalled at the effects of the Industrial
Revolution on the life of his England and condemned what
he called the "dark Satanic Mills." Both men would oppose
the life-deadening and life-denying aspects of the modern
world, both would oppose what Freud calls Thanatos, the
death instinct. Blake mythicizes that aspect of man's makeup
with a group of twelve lost creatures called the Sons of Albion,
who personify an "Abstract objecting power that Negatives
everything" (*Jerusalem*, 10:7); Tolkien feels that his myth of
Sauron expresses an impulse in the cosmos itself, an even
greater malice of which he is but the "servant or emissary"
(III, p. 155). Both men assume that the struggle against evil
is an inevitable part of life: Blake always felt that "Without
Contraries is no progression" (*The Marriage of Heaven and
Hell*), and Tolkien acknowledges that there may always be
Saurons to fight (III, p. 155). The difference lies in the ground
on which they stand to combat the evil, the assumptions
from which they start. Blake assumes that the fundamental
struggle is between Thanatos and desirably unfettered Eros,
while Tolkien is convinced that unfettered Eros is the ally,
even the servant, of Thanatos.

What we can perhaps be most thankful for is that each
myth is altogether suitable to the age out of which it comes.

The world of the French and American Revolutions, which Blake addressed, deeply needed the freeing explosion of Orc; the world Tolkien addresses, faced with the altogether unprecedented cultural facts described by Blackmur, needs another mythology, and Tolkien has given us the most useful one I know, though we are well advised to be critical in our acceptance of some parts of it.

TOLKIEN'S WORLD

The Structure and Aesthetic of
The Lord of the Rings

A poet, they say, must follow *Nature;* and by Nature we
are to suppose can only be meant the known and experienced course of affairs in this world. Whereas the poet
has a world of his own, where experience has less to do,
than consistent imagination.

He has, besides, a supernatural world to range in. He
has Gods, and Faeries, and Witches at his command: and,
     . . . *O! who can tell*
   The hidden pow'r *of herbes, and might of magic spell?*
                 Spenser, B. 1 C. 2
Thus in the poet's world, all is marvellous and extraor-
dinary; yet not *unnatural* in one sense, as it agrees to the
conceptions that are readily entertained of these magical
and wonder-working natures.

                    — RICHARD HURD,
            Letters on Chivalry and Romance

WE WILL MISJUDGE *The Lord of the Rings* unless we grant
that the aesthetic principles governing a fantasy world
are different both from the laws of our own realm of common-sense reality and from those governing "realistic" literature. The world of fantasy is a world of desire fulfilled,
of beauty past describing, of goodness and wickedness past
defiling or redeeming: a world in clear and perilous danger
of sliding into merest wish-fulfillment and sentimentality.

The author of a successful fantasy will need a strong self-discipline, analogous to but opposite from that required of the realistic author. Realism (I use the term in its widest and most general sense) has its own kind of sentimentality (as in Socialist Realism, where character and incident serve not their own purposes but that of ideology), and the greater the sentimentality, the closer "realism" slides toward fantasy. Just as realism can degenerate into fantasy, so fantasy can degenerate into realism, as in the "dream frame" that an author may feel is necessary to explain how his fantasy might have happened. My point is that fantasy literature is based on an aesthetic as demanding and uncompromising as any realism. The realistic writer must, to maintain his credibility, make clear (however implicitly) how his events *could* have happened, for realism stands upon an ontology that grants reality only on a basis of cause-and-effect sequences. Fantasy stands upon a different theory of reality, but one demanding with equal rigor that the fantasist keep always in mind his aesthetic principles: that what happens in his world accord not with his daydreams nor with our own world's laws of common sense, but with the peculiar laws of the sub-created cosmos.

Tolkien himself introduces the beginnings of a critical notion about fantasy ontology in his essay "On Fairy-Stories." Discussing Coleridge's conception of the "willing suspension of disbelief . . . which constitutes poetic faith" (*Biographia Literaria,* Chapter XIV), Tolkien suggests a counter theory: "What really happens is that the story-maker proves a successful 'sub-creator.' He makes a Secondary World which your mind can enter. Inside it, what he relates is 'true': it accords with the laws of that world. You therefore believe it, while you are, as it were, inside." The reader of fantasy needs, in order to remain inside the Secondary World, not a negative suspension of *dis*belief, but a positive form of "Secondary Belief" that must be the product of the author's art. For the "moment disbelief arises, the spell is broken; the magic, or rather art, has failed. You are then out in the Primary World again, looking at the little abortive Secondary World from outside" (TL, p. 37).

The disciplined fantasist must, therefore, in order to maintain Secondary Belief, always keep an eye to the structural principles, the internal laws, of the world he is creating, for his is a delicate art, and perhaps more than any other has a set of limitations requiring absolute respect. The limitations, however, bring their own kind of freedom, the greatest perhaps being the enormous range in the *kind* of experiences the fantasist can present (fighting dragons, becoming invisible), a freedom limited only by the way the characters can react to these experiences. Realistic art involves just the opposite sort of difficulty; it can present only a limited range of experiences — those "believable" according to common-sense reality — but it has great freedom in the tremendous range of possible responses to the experience. All this results in two rather simple principles of narrative construction: within the laws of the forms, in realism action is limited, reaction infinite, in fantasy action is infinite, reaction limited.

Since fantasy characters react for the most part only as heroes or villains, wise men or fools, the value of a work of fantasy depends not on the possibilities of *reaction,* but on the richness and quality of *action.* Judging the richness or multiplicity of action is not difficult; even a superficial reader can quickly decide whether there is enough meat in a book to justify continuing. More difficult, and what must engage the critical reader of fantasy, is the *quality* of the action. This chapter will attempt to show that the quality and value of the narrative in fantasy literature is dependent upon the richness and complexity of the interrelationships between the action, on the one hand, and the internal laws or structural principles of the fantasy world, on the other. The success of fantasy is determined by how imaginatively, consistently, and coherently the author can work within the combination of freedoms and limitations governing a fantasy world. "Internal laws" are the physics and metaphysics of the Secondary World, and since every fantasy is a new creation, a new world limited only by the imaginative powers of its creator, each work of fantasy must be judged by its own internal complexities. The critic of fantasy must discover and formulate the internal laws of the Secondary World he is examining in order fully to understand the narrative principles of its fictional action and to judge the success with which it fulfills its aims. Here are the internal laws of Middle-earth:

(1) The cosmos is providentially controlled.

(2) Intention structures results. That is, Middle-earth's moral structure works according to a kind of "truth table": $+ \times + = +; - \times - = +$ (a good action with a good intent will have a good result; an evil action with an evil intent will also have an ultimately good result).

(3) Moral and magical law have the force of physical law.

(4) Will and states of mind, both evil and good, can have objective reality and physical energy.

(5) All experience is the realization of proverbial truth.

These laws overlap in their effects, and some might even be subsumed under others, but I have stated them separately for clarity. They are, however, rather abstract, so I shall give some initial examples of how they work.

(1) Perhaps the clearest example of the workings of Middle-earthly Providence is in Gandalf's remark to Frodo about the discovery of the Ring: "I can put it no plainer than by saying that Bilbo was *meant* to find the Ring, and *not* by its maker. In which case you also were *meant* to have it. And that may be an encouraging thought" (I, p. 65). Tolkien never clearly states the source of the providential control in the narrative of the *Rings*, though we can gather from Appendix A that Middle-earth's divine hierarchy consists of "the Valar, the Guardians of the World" (III, p. 315), who are, in turn, responsible to "the One" (III, p. 317).

(2) In Middle-earth, the result of an action is the product of its intent. Here is perhaps the basic difference between the moral structures of Tolkien's world and our own. We know that intention has nothing to do with result, but Tolkien's Secondary World is so finely structured by moral law that the meaning of all its actions is reducible to the terms of a mathematical truth table. When, for example, Frodo tells Gandalf it was "a pity that Bilbo did not stab that vile creature [Gollum], when he had a chance," Gandalf replies that all the rest of Bilbo's life and the events of the *Rings* will be positively affected by that one act: "Pity? It was Pity that stayed his hand. Pity, and Mercy: not to strike without need. And he has been well rewarded, Frodo. Be sure that he took so little hurt from the evil, and escaped in the end, because he began his ownership of the Ring so" (I, pp. 68-69).

(3) That the moral law works in Tolkien's world as inexorably as gravity is clear from the preceding; that magic is as real in Middle-earth is equally apparent from the Ring itself. With the One Ring, we are at the very source of Tolkien's own imaginative ponderings about the structuring

principles of Middle-earth. What indeed are the moral and physical implications of wearing a ring that makes a person invisible? A world in which such a thing exists will have a vastly different set of physical laws from those of our own, and working them out will require a great deal of imaginative thought. As Tolkien has said, it is easy to make up a green sun; the difficulty begins when we try to make up a world in which a green sun makes sense. Consider the moral implications of the power of invisibility and you will begin to construct your own Secondary World.

(4) That states of mind and will can have physical power, affecting others at a distance, is apparent from the "force field" of terror surrounding a Nazgûl. As Aragorn says, their power is in terror; one need only fly overhead, and all beneath shrink in fear and loss of will.

(5) As Mircea Eliade has pointed out, the world of the mythic imagination deals not merely with local and unrelated happenings, but with "categories of events"; where there is a hero, there is also inevitably a reptilian monster: the thing does not work any other way. The same is true in the imaginative world of Middle-earth; according to its fantasy ontology, only those events have reality that reproduce what Eliade calls an "archetypal gesture" [1] — the primordial categories of human experience and desire — categories reducible in Middle-earth to proverbial truth. In other words, the archetypal patterns of events that are realized in fantasy as conventions of romance literature (heroes fighting monsters) are the way things have *always* happened from the perspective of Middle-earth's inhabitants, and their proverbs describe those events. Théoden, for example, moralizes that *"oft evil will shall evil mar"* (II, p. 200), and surely enough, here lies the moral heart of the action in Book III, as we shall see.

The rest of this chapter will be an attempt to show that the pattern of the action in each of the six books of *The Lord of the Rings* is dependent upon the workings of some or all of these laws, for things happen in Middle-earth, as in our own world, in keeping with its physics and metaphysics.

The events of Book I, and consequently the rest of the story, stem from Bilbo's act of mercy and pity in *The Hobbit* — his sparing of Gollum's life — an act that sets up the possibility of Frodo's inheriting and bearing the Ring, and an act wholly in keeping with the merciful Providence Gandalf later perceives at work in the entire process. Gandalf's (and probably Tolkien's) only inkling of a larger meaning and purpose in the finding of the Ring in the earlier story comes in his remark to Bilbo at the very end when he says that his adventures were not "managed by mere luck" (*Hobbit*, p. 317). But there is no sense in *The Hobbit* itself that this is the case; as we have seen already, the larger implications in Tolkien's children's book are rare indeed. Gandalf's final remark to Bilbo reads more like the beginning of Tolkien's own recognition of the larger possibilities of the magic ring, the beginning of a process of imaginative growth quickly finding fruition in *The Hobbit*'s sequel. In *The Lord of the Rings* it becomes evident in the second chapter (written, we recall, even before *The Hobbit* was published) that the workings of Providence will be basic to the narrative when Gandalf tells Frodo he was "*meant* to have" the Ring. Gandalf's statement parallels Elrond's in Book II that "this task is appointed for" Frodo (I, p. 284). Frodo's responses to these challenges to his will and courage are the formative moments, the seeds, from which come the actions of Books I and II, for Frodo's hobbit courage and self-effacement provide the moral force behind the adventures of the first two books. There are, in other words, two moral laws of Middle-earth at work in Books I and II (Law One, the cosmos is providential, and Law Two, intent structures action). And since such laws are part of a "romantic" rather than a "realistic" cosmos, the fifth law is likewise at work in both books; both are structured according to the conventional or archetypal pattern of the quest romance. Northrop Frye has described the pattern in these terms: "as soon as romance achieves a literary form it tends to limit itself to a sequence of minor adventures leading up to a major or climacteric adventure, usually announced from the beginning, the completion of which rounds off the story." [2] In Book I there are six of these minor or "preliminary" adventures, as I call them; each involves a major threat to the Ring and Ringbearer, and in each Frodo is saved by the providential appearance or action of an outside force or helper. In the course of his preliminary adventures on the road from Hobbiton to Rivendell, Frodo is tested and toughened, is first wounded and draws first blood, gradually learning he has indeed the courage to be Ringbearer. The first two adventures teach him enough fortitude and presence of mind that in the last four his own strength of heart and will are partly responsible for the happy outcome. The purpose of his preliminary adventures, then, is to allow Frodo to grow sufficiently in heroic stature on his own and learn enough about himself and the world so that he will be able to make his fateful decision at the Council of Elrond to bear the Ring to Mount Doom. He learns self-reliance while traveling from his home to Rivendell without the help of Gandalf, who later tells him, "I was delayed . . . and that nearly proved our ruin. And yet I am not sure: it may have been better so" (I, p. 232). A look at Frodo's six preliminary adventures will show him growing slowly but steadily to heroic stature.

In Book I, the real threat of the Black Riders is that they may frighten Frodo into putting on the Ring and thereby entering their realm and power, the dominion of Sauron. In the first preliminary adventure, the lone Rider, attracted by the smell of Frodo's fear, stalks the hobbit, who is cowering by the roadside. Indeed the Rider's only physical sense is smell; Tolkien is probably drawing here on Heraclitus' notion that the souls in Hades, being but smoke, know each other only by scent. The Wraiths can "see" only someone who is wearing the Ring, and Frodo nearly gives himself away at the beginning:

> Frodo thought he heard the sound of snuffling. The shadow bent to the ground, and then began to crawl towards him. Once more the desire to slip on the Ring came over Frodo; but this time it was stronger than before. So strong that, almost before he realized what he was doing, his hand was groping in his pocket (I, p. 88).

Frodo would at that moment have been taken had not a group of Elves appeared, beings who rarely entered the Shire: "there came a sound like mingled song and laughter. Clear voices rose and fell in the starlit air. The black shadow straightened up and retreated" (I, p. 88). In this first adventure, Frodo must be helped by a purely providential event, for he has yet to learn his primary lesson, one best stated by Elrond: "There is naught that you can do, other than to resist, with hope or without it" (I, p. 255).

In their first preliminary adventure, both Frodo and Sam take their initial steps forward in preparation for the major quest. After the Rider has fled at the appearance of the Elves, the hobbits join them for supper. As they talk, Frodo learns from Gildor that he was indeed wise to leave Hobbiton when he did: " . . . it seems to me that you have set out only just in time, if indeed you are in time. You must now make haste, and neither stay nor turn back; for the Shire is no longer any protection to you" (I, p. 93). In this conversation Frodo makes explicit to himself for the first time what he most needs to be Ringbearer, what he did not have in the first adventure and what he must learn in the next five: "But where shall I find courage? . . . That is what I chiefly need." Gildor's answer hints that it will be found in the only place it will do any good, in Frodo's own hobbit heart: "Courage is found in unlikely places" (I, p. 94).

Sam, too, exhibits notable growth after the first adventure and gives strong proof of his maturation early in the second. The sight of Elves has been one of his deepest wishes, and having seen them at last, he quietly reflects:

> "They seem a bit above my likes and dislikes, so to speak," answered Sam slowly. "It don't seem to matter what I think about them. They are quite different from what I expected — so old and young, and so gay and sad, as it were."
>
> Frodo looked at Sam rather startled, half expecting to see some outward sign of the odd change that seemed to have come over him . . .
>
> "Yes, sir. I don't know how to say it, but after last night I feel different . . . I have something to do before the end, and it lies ahead . . . I must see it through" (I, p. 96).

Later Sam is to repeat these very words "I must see it through" at the darkest moment of the quest, when Frodo lies apparently dead of the poison of Shelob. The Halfling gardener goes on to attempt the completion of the quest himself, the culmination of heroic growth that began in the first adventure.

The earliest outward sign of Sam's worth appears in the second preliminary adventure, when he saves the charmed and sleeping Frodo from Old Man Willow. Here as in the first adventure, Frodo is powerless to act in his own defense, requiring help from both a rapidly maturing Sam and Tom Bombadil. The hobbits, timidly attempting a short cut through the Old Forest to avoid the Black Riders, are drawn into "a course chosen for them" (I, p. 126) by the malicious will of Old Man Willow. Frodo must learn by hard experience the wisdom Elrond later summarizes at the Council: the way that "seems easiest . . . must be shunned . . . Now at this last we must take a hard road, a road unforeseen" (I, p. 280). The directing will of the forest is, as it were, an objectification of the hobbits' own lack of will; they must learn that whatever one does not do for himself, Sauron, or those equally malicious, will do.

Drawn to the foot of the gigantic Willow, Merry and Pippin are ingested and Frodo is pitched into the river. Sam manages to rescue Frodo but can do nothing for the other two, so the elder hobbit panics, running "along the path crying *help! help! help!*" (I, p. 130). Tom Bombadil comes immediately to the rescue, commanding the tree to release Merry and Pippin. But strangely, Tom had not heard Frodo's cry; he was merely returning that way from an errand. Tom's arrival is purely providential, necessary because the hobbits have yet to grow sufficiently to help themselves and because his instructions are vital to the continuation of the quest. For under the tutelage of Tom Bombadil, Frodo is taught another lesson, which he could never have learned on his own in the domesticated, well-protected Shire: he discovers the malice implicit in the cosmos, malice entirely independent of Sauron and of which he is only the personified though immensely powerful spirit. As Frodo had learned from the Elves the necessary and sobering information that not even the Shire remained safe from the inroads of Sauron's servants, so he now learns from Tom that even in the realm of nature (that in the Shire seemed tame and fat) there are both "evil things and good things, things friendly and things unfriendly, cruel things and kind things, and secrets hidden under brambles." Of the trees especially Frodo learns that "countless years had filled them with pride and rooted wisdom, and with malice" (I, p. 141). But outweighing even his grasp of the duplicity of nature is Frodo's learning from Tom the ultimate impotence of evil. The Ring cannot render Tom invisible; he makes *it* vanish and reappear (I, p. 144).

Tom Bombadil, Frodo's mentor in this second adventure, is Tolkien's version of the stock figure Northrop Frye calls the "Golux" (after Thurber), the one romance character who can "elude the moral antithesis of heroism and villainy" pervasive in romance, one of the "spirits of nature . . . [who] represent partly the moral neutrality of the intermediate world of nature and partly a world of mystery." [3] Tom's "moral neutrality" is attested by Gandalf, when Elrond ponders whether he should have invited Tom to the Council: "He would not have come," says Gandalf, for such matters as the Ring and the battles fought over it have "no power over him." Even if he were given the Ring itself, "he would soon forget it, or most likely throw it away" (I, pp. 278–79).

As embodiment of nature's moral neutrality or ambiguity, Tom is the ideal figure to initiate Frodo into knowledge of Middle-earth's implicit malice. The Ringbearer must learn to deal with both faces of the nonhuman in Tolkien's world, and the adventure with Tom and Old Man Willow schools him well; by the time of the third adventure he has grown noticeably, exhibiting for the first time his newly awakened courage, striking off the hand of the Barrow-wight to save his friends.

The adventure of the Barrow-downs summons what Frodo most needs to complete the quest, his hobbit courage: "There is a seed of courage hidden (often deeply, it is true) in the heart of the fattest and most timid hobbit, waiting for some final and desperate danger to make it grow" (I, p. 151). Frodo learns in his encounter with the Wight that he can be at the same time "angry and afraid" (I, p. 151) — a discovery each warrior must make in his own way — and that at the last resort love for his friends can banish fear and arouse courage. When he awakens inside the barrow and sees his companions about to be beheaded, he first thinks of putting on the Ring and escaping, "grieving for Merry, and Sam, and Pippin, but free and alive himself . . . But the courage that had been awakened in him was now too strong" (I, p. 152). Frodo strikes off the spectral hand, and remembering Tom's advice, cries for help. Bombadil as promised appears immediately.

Frodo's fourth, fifth, and sixth preliminary adventures require less commentary. The fourth takes place at *The Prancing Pony*, Barliman Butterbur's inn at Bree. Here, Frodo retains elements of his hobbit carelessness (allowing himself and his friends to be drawn into the barroom *bavardage*), but tries valiantly to act with dispatch in preventing Pippin's drunken tale of Bilbo's party and mysterious disappearance; in doing so, however, he lets the Ring slip onto his finger, vanishing to the puzzlement of the Breelanders and the knowing eye of Bill Ferny. Only the providential appearance of Strider saves him from the consequence, the midnight raid on the hobbits' room.

In Frodo's fifth preliminary adventure, at Weathertop, the gradually maturing hobbit is foolish and courageous in about equal proportions, putting on the Ring in his fear of the Riders, but also fighting back to the end, striking at the Wraith and shouting "*O Elbereth! Gilthoniel!*" (I, p. 208). Frodo's spur-of-the-moment act briefly discomfits the Rider attacking him, and as Gandalf says later, "fortune or fate have helped you,. . . not to mention courage . . . only your shoulder was pierced; and that was because you resisted to the last" (I, p. 234).

Finally, in the sixth adventure at the Ford of Bruinen, Frodo exhibits to the full the heroism he has with great difficulty wrung from his preceding experiences; he refuses to don the Ring and shouts defiance, sword in hand, even as he faints from the poison of the Morgul knife. The miraculous assistance of Gandalf and Glorfindel then keeps him safe to Rivendell, as they drown the black horses and discomfit their ghastly riders.

The Secondary World of fantasy is a world of coherence and relationship; heroic actions, transpiring in keeping with the limited and exacting laws of the created world, are most often parallel in form and exhibited in narrative patterns that are themselves parallel. This becomes especially clear in Book II, the narrative of which closely duplicates that of Book I. As I is the preliminary adventure of the four hobbits, II presents the parallel adventures of the Nine Walkers. In both books, the Ringbearer and his companions proceed from a sheltered place, through perilous adventures, to a center of elvish retreat (Hobbiton to Rivendell, Rivendell to Lórien).

Frodo accepts the company of a man associated with Gondor (Aragorn its true king in I, Boromir heir of its steward in II), who must decide whether to take the Ring or aid the quest. In both cases the decision precedes Frodo's putting on the Ring (or allowing it to slip on) and thereby risking all to Sauron (in the episodes at *The Prancing Pony* and Parth Galen). The two books are parallel in their structures as well as their episodes. Both begin in festivity (Bilbo's birthday party, the feasting at Rivendell) and continue in a second chapter with lengthy scenes of initiating information ("The Shadow of the Past" in Book I, in which Gandalf tells Frodo all he knows of the Ring; "The Council of Elrond" in Book II, in which the full history of the Ring is recounted). After the narrative of its history the Ring is revealed (the test by fire in I, Frodo's displaying the Ring to the Council in II) and Frodo makes his fateful decision as Ringbearer. At this point in both books Frodo learns that he was fated to bear the Ring (Gandalf declares in I that it was "meant" he should have it; Elrond announces in II that "this task is appointed for" Frodo). Finally, in both books, the Ringbearer's companions are chosen (Merry, Pippin, and Sam in I, the Nine Walkers in II). There follows, in the second half of each book, a sequence of adventures ending in a separation at a river (Bruinen, Anduin).

The two sets of adventures on the road also are parallel to a remarkable degree. The pursuit by the Black Riders in I is comparable to the pursuit of the Fellowship by a large flock of black crows in II. The adventure in the Old Forest in which the hobbits learn of the deep malice within nature (personified in Old Man Willow) closely matches the account in Book II of the attempt to cross the pass of Caradhras, in which again the malice of the mountain (independent of Sauron, like the Willow) endangers the life of the Ringbearer and, like the Old Forest, redirects the path of the Ring. Sam's saving Frodo from the root and the water in Book I closely matches his rescuing him from the arm of the Watcher in the water in Book II. The episode of the Barrow-wight in I is parallel in a very important way to the passage through Moria in II; in both accounts Frodo exhibits great courage by stabbing with his sword, first at the hand of the Wight, then at the foot of the cave troll. In each scene, Frodo is underground, apparently trapped, and terrified, and in each, he saves the day with his courage and quick action. The episode at Weathertop in Book I in which Frodo disastrously puts on the Ring and barely escapes capture closely parallels the adventure at Amon Hen in Book II, when Frodo again puts on the Ring in his attempt to escape the crazed Boromir and is nearly caught by the spectral hand of Sauron. Finally, the adventure at the Ford of Bruinen, in which Frodo's will and courage stand the final test in Book I, closely parallels the hobbit's courageous decision on the banks of the Anduin in Book II to go it alone. Entering or crossing a river is of course an ancient symbol for a final initiation or last irreversible step, and both books end with Frodo's "crossing his Rubicon," giving conclusive evidence that he does indeed have the will and courage to be Ringbearer.

By the end of Book II, Frodo's preliminary adventures are over, and the real quest, alone with Sam, begins in earnest. The adventures of Book I stripped Frodo of his hobbit fears and complacencies, leaving him naked with his hobbit courage. Book II must strip him further, as one by one the Nine Walkers fall away: Gandalf vanishes in Moria, Aragorn becomes, for the moment, an indecisive leader, Boromir succumbs to his lust for the Ring's power, Merry and Pippin, Orc-back, speed toward Fangorn.

The parallel plot-lines of Book III, the awakenings of the Ents by Merry and Pippin to destroy Isengard and of Théoden by Gandalf to battle Saruman, are both structured by the laws of providential control and of the cause-and-effect morality. And, true to the internal meanings of Tolkien's world, the two actions have proverbial significance. The plot-line of the hobbits is summed up by two analogous proverbs: Gandalf's "Often does hatred hurt itself" (II, p. 190) and Théoden's *"oft evil will shall evil mar"* (II, p. 200), and the Aragorn-Gandalf plot-line in a single proverb, Éomer's "oft the unbidden guest proves the best company" (II, p. 140).

Book III presents the adventures of one-half the sundered company — all except Sam and Frodo. Book II ended with Frodo severed from his companions, fulfilling Elrond's decree that only the Ringbearer had final responsibility for the quest. As it turns out, however, and as Elrond did not foresee, the actions of the sundered group are as necessary to the overall quest as Frodo's journey itself. For the two major victories of Book III, over Saruman at Isengard and over the Orcs at Helm's Deep, must precede Rohan's ride to Gondor. The battle at Gondor must likewise engage Sauron's attention while Frodo and Sam creep toward Orodruin; but more of this later. In the meantime, these two necessary victories result from evil intentions upon innocent creatures; both stem from Saruman's greedy attempt to capture hobbits at Parth Galen. In the plan of Book III, it is imperative that Merry and Pippin reach Fangorn and arouse Treebeard. On their own, however, they could never have crossed the forty-five leagues from Parth Galen to Fangorn in the mere three days' time they have. What gets them there, of course, is the reversed effects of the evil intent of Saruman, who has sent out a raiding party of Uruk-hai to capture hobbits and bring them back to Isengard for torture and questioning. We remember, too, that the second book ended with Boromir's inadvertently forcing Frodo's necessary decision to set out alone for Mordor, necessary since the company had to be separated so that Merry and Pippin on the one hand and Aragorn, Legolas, and Gimli on the other could perform their vital roles in the quest. Again, Frodo's decision and the consequent necessary separation of the Nine Walkers was precipitated by an evil action — Boromir's attempt, parallel to Saruman's, to wrest the Ring from its bearer. "*Oft evil will shall evil mar.*"

At the beginning of Book III, as the result of the inadvertently joined evil wills of Saruman and Boromir, Frodo and Sam go one way, Merry and Pippin the other. This leaves the remainder of the company with a hard choice; as Aragorn says, "if I seek [Frodo] now in the wilderness, I must abandon the captives to torment and death. My heart speaks clearly at last: the fate of the Bearer is in my hands no longer. The Company has played its part" (II, p. 21). This decision, made in pity and loyalty, can have none other than a positive effect, for in following, however fruitlessly, after their two small friends, the three hunters must come across Éomer and, more importantly, Gandalf, thereby beginning to play their vital roles in the battle of Helm's Deep. More important yet, by going in the right direction to meet Gandalf, Aragorn is thus present with the wizard at the flinging of the *palantír*, making it possible for him to claim it as his rightful property and later use it to precipitate the victory of Pelennor Fields.

Aragorn follows the young hobbits, speeding toward Isengard, but right at the edge of Fangorn, as it happens, the Orc party is overtaken by a band of Rohirrim, bent on destroying the trespassers in their land. It is inevitable that Merry and Pippin die in the confusion of battle, except for one thing, and again an evil act has a good result; for Grishnákh, seeing that his Orcs are surrounded, attempts to spirit away Merry and Pippin for his own gain. He is providentially killed (and Tolkien makes the nature of the good fortune clear), while the hobbits escape, to make their way to Fangorn and their fated meeting with Treebeard: as the Orc creeps through the Rohirrim encirclement, he comes in the dark upon one of the horsemen; he flings himself flat, drawing his sword and meaning to "kill his captives, rather than allow them to escape or to be rescued." The very evil of his intent betrays him, for the sword "rang faintly, and glinted a little in the light of the fire away to his left. An arrow came whistling out of the gloom: it was aimed with skill, or guided by fate, and it pierced his right hand." Grishnákh screams and is run down and speared, while the hobbits, in their elven cloaks, remain unseen. Again, their innocence and the influence of the cloaks protect them when a horseman of Rohan comes to the aid of his comrade who has shot the Orc. The horse comes directly at the prostrate pair of hobbits, but whether because "of some special keenness of sight, or because of some other sense, the horse lifted and sprang lightly over them" (II, p. 60). "*Oft evil will shall evil mar,*" or, as Gandalf later says, "So between them our enemies have contrived only to bring Merry and Pippin with marvellous speed, and in the nick of time, to Fangorn, where otherwise they would never have come at all" (II, p. 101).

Once inside the forest, the hobbits make their way to the top of a hill, the very spot where Treebeard often comes "when his mind is uneasy," says Gandalf later, "and rumours of the world outside trouble him" (II, p. 103). The smoke of the Rohirrim cremation of the Orcs has especially troubled him, already near to rage as he is over Saruman's despoiling of his trees, and the news the young hobbits bring completes his anger. He is so angry, in fact, he comes near to killing them both on sight; only their obvious innocence, especially their chattering voices, saves them: "if I had seen you, before I heard your voices . . . nice little voices . . . I should have just trodden on you, taking you for little Orcs" (II, p. 67).

Having befriended the hobbits he takes them to his home, where his hospitality plays a major role in their future, for the Entdraught Treebeard serves them causes their growth to un-hobbitlike proportions: "I can give you a drink," he says, "that will keep you green and growing for a long, long while" (II, p. 70). Little do they realize that his meaning is literal; the Entdraught causes Merry and Pippin to grow in the next few months taller than the Old Bullroarer, the first hobbit to top four feet and ride a horse. Their growth both metaphorically and literally to heroic stature begins with the drink that makes "the hair on their heads . . . [stand] up, waving and curling and growing" (II, p. 74).

The second major action in Book III parallels the first both in theme and outcome, being structured by the same laws of Middle-earth. Just as Merry and Pippin providentially arrive at the right moment to awaken Treebeard from his Entish unhastiness to battle Saruman, so Gandalf providentially comes back — beyond hope and at greatest need — to awaken Théoden from his aged despair to make war on the White Wizard. Together, with Gandalf's aid, the Ents and

Rohirrim win the first battle of the great war against Sauron, a battle set precipitously in motion by the greedy haste of Saruman. Like the Merry-Pippin strand of Book III, this strand as well is the realization of proverbial truth. Just after Gimli saves Éomer from a group of Orcs outside Hornburggates, his friend thanks him, declaring that "oft the unbidden guest proves the best company" (II, p. 140). This proverb sums up the Gandalf-Aragorn section of the narrative of Book III. Gandalf returns unbidden and even unwelcome to Meduseld, reviving the spirit and hope of Théoden; the unbidden Gimli saves Éomer; the unbidden Huorns turn the tide of battle at Helm's Deep; and, in an inverse way, the unbidden guest Wormtongue at Orthanc proves the "best" company at the tower, not for Saruman, but for those outside, as he flings down in his hatred the *palantír*, the most valuable object in all of Saruman's realm.

This is the final important action in Book III relating to the theme of the reversed effects of evil intent. Wormtongue's act does indeed set off a chain of events that not even Gandalf could have foreseen, for the major events of Book V stem from this one moment. The great war of Gondor was precipitated by a combination of Wormtongue's hatred and Sauron's greedy haste, coupled with a little hobbit's curiosity, for Pippin, fascinated by the beautiful stone, cannot resist peeping into it, revealing its true importance. Aragorn then takes what is his own and decides in Book V to reveal himself as King to Sauron. Unnerved by what he sees, Sauron turns his attention from his own land and, before his armies are fully ready, strikes at Gondor in the hope of a quick victory over its returned King, thus allowing Frodo and Sam to slip unnoticed across Gorgoroth. And it all began with Wormtongue's evil wish.

The events of Book IV happen in keeping with three of the internal laws of Middle-earth, the laws of providential control, of the external force of will, and of the reversed effects of evil intentions. This book is, in a sense, Frodo and Sam's version of Merry and Pippin's adventure in Book III, for just as it is essential that the minor pair of hobbits (as I call them) cross Rohan in three days, and succeed only because of the evil will of Saruman, so in Book IV the major pair must cross the Dead Marshes and enter Mordor, and they succeed only because of the reversed effects of Gollum's lust for the Ring and the positive effects of Frodo's good will (combined, of course, with other factors, among them Sauron's distracted attention).

Tolkien establishes his theme for Book IV with Frodo's words to Sam while they are yet on the seemingly impassable ridges of the Emyn Muil: "It's my doom, I think, to go to that Shadow yonder, so that a way will be found. But will good or evil show it to me?" (II, p. 210). As it turns out, *both* good and evil, both Sméagol and Gollum, show him the way. Gollum's lust for the Ring has kept him on Frodo's trail since the company entered Moria on January 13. He follows Frodo across the Emyn Muil until the night of February 29 (the same day Merry and Pippin meet Tree-beard), when in the darkness he slips and falls right into Sam's arms. And the time is propitious. Frodo has just realized he has taken the wrong turn, that he should have "come down from the North, east of the River and of the Emyn Muil" (II, p. 210), but now it is too late, for the east side of Anduin is lined with prowling Orcs. The future of the quest looks dim indeed until, into their very midst, falls the only creature in all Middle-earth who knows the "one way across [the Dead Marshes] between the North-end and the South-end" (II, p. 225) — Gollum, drawn by his need for the Ring. Frodo, sword in hand, finds himself with the same opportunity to kill the wretched creature that Bilbo had seventy-eight years before (and with the same weapon, Sting). Once again, just as Bilbo's pity and mercy spared Gollum and "rule[d] the fate of many" (I, p. 69), Frodo's not least, so will Frodo's pity and mercy save the quest. The good effects of his grace resurrect Sméagol to convey them across the Dead Marshes: "you must help us, if you can. One good turn deserves another" — the structuring proverb for Book IV. Gollum answers, "Yes, yes, indeed . . . We will come with them. Find them safe paths in the dark" (II, p. 222). So for a while, "The hobbits were . . . wholly in the hands of Gollum" (II, p. 232).

The realized proverbial effect of Frodo's "good turn" lasts to the eastern edge of the Dead Marshes; Gollum remains Sméagol until he reaches the borders of Mordor, when the evil of that land reinfects his heart. Just before the three pass into Sauron's domain, a Ringwraith flies overhead on some mission of evil, flinging them onto the ground with the force-field of terror that surrounds him: "From that time on Sam thought that he sensed a change in Gollum again" (II, p. 237). After this point, the Ring grows heavier around Frodo's neck and Sméagol gives way to Gollum, who begins forming his plan to deliver the Ringbearer to Shelob: "She might help. She might, yes" (II, p. 241).

To this point, the "good" that Frodo hoped for on Emyn Muil has led them; now the "evil" must do so. He sees Morannon and realizes it is impassable. Then Gollum, his Sméagol-part defunct in Mordor, whispers, "There is another way" (II, p. 246) — Shelob's tunnel. It is of course quite literally the only other way into Mordor, and the only force capable of leading them there is the evil will of Gollum, who hopes that when Shelob throws away the empty clothes of the Ringbearer, she will also discard the Precious.

Lying between Morannon and Cirith Ungol, however, is Ithilien and an adventure essential to the other half of the quest. For the major pair must meet Faramir in Ithilien, just as the minor must meet Treebeard in Fangorn. Indeed, as this might lead us to suspect, Book IV closely parallels Book III in narrative pattern, as II parallels I. In each book of the second volume, a hobbit pair must traverse a seemingly impossible distance (III) or impassable area (IV) in a limited amount of time, and in each, they succeed only because of the reversed effects of evil intentions upon them (Saruman's, Gollum's). After the crossing, each hobbit pair encounters a figure of authority in a forbidden land (Treebeard in Fangorn, Faramir in Ithilien), who has been drawn there by rumor of enemy encroachment on his territory and led to the specific location of the hobbits in each case by the sight of smoke (the Orc cremation, Sam's cook-fire). In each case, that leader must decide whether to kill or help the hobbits. He decides in both instances to help, but the decision to kill is narrowly averted by the wise and generous refusal to act hastily (Treebeard declares that he had nearly "trodden on" the minor pair, taking them for "little Orcs"; Faramir tells Sam, "Were I as hasty as you, I might have slain you long ago" [II, p. 273]). After parleying, the hobbits proceed with the authority figure to his cave, where they get their first good meal and safe rest in a long while. The hobbit pairs then proceed on their quests, each of which ends in the destruction of a dark tower (Orthanc, Barad-dûr).

The encounter with Faramir is an essential moment in the quest, with implications not only for the major pair's success in Gorgoroth (they get enough food from him to eke out their supply of *lembas* to the Crack of Doom) but for Gandalf's role as well. Faramir must see Frodo so that he can later tell Gandalf the hobbits are still alive and proceeding toward Mordor, in order that Gandalf, in his turn, may know that there is hope in continuing to distract Sauron's attention from his own land; thus the "foolish" attack on Morannon Gate in Book VI. And of course what brings Frodo and Faramir together is the smoke of Sam's cooking-fire, a fire prepared in Sam's loving concern for his starved master: " 'Too thin and drawn he is,' he muttered. 'Not right for a hobbit. If I can get these coneys cooked, I'm going to wake him up' " (II, p. 261).

The major action of Book V is the great war of Gondor. The narrative, however, centers not around the great defenders of the city, men like Denethor and Faramir, nor even the most powerful characters, Gandalf and Aragorn, but rather around the weakest and most foolish, Merry and Pippin. The four hobbits continue to fulfill the words of Elrond at the Council: "This is the hour of the Shire-folk, when they arise from their quiet fields to shake the towers and counsels of the great" (I, p. 284). Book V is about the minor pair in much the way Book III has been; indeed the events in V stem directly from a single action in III — Pippin's peering into the *palantír*. The war of Gondor, like the war of Rohan, was precipitated by a hobbit.

Book V presents two parallel plot-lines — Merry's and Pippin's — each of whom swears fealty to a king (Pippin to Denethor, Merry to Théoden) and each of whom through his loyalty saves the life of the king's child (Merry, Éowyn, and Pippin, Faramir), after which, most properly, Faramir and Éowyn marry, thus uniting forever the preserved lines of Gondor and Rohan.

Two proverbs structure the Merry-Pippin plot-line, and each is stated soon after the hobbits swear loyalty to their respective lords, Théoden and Denethor, whose names, incidentally, are virtual anagrams of each other. The proverbs are Gandalf's and Éowyn's; their realization as action stands at the narrative heart of Book V: "generous deed should not be checked by cold counsel" (III, p. 32); "*Where will wants not, a way opens*" (III, p. 77). These comments, made in both cases by the person who carries each hobbit to Gondor from Rohan, concern the moral implications of the hobbits' impulsive gifts of loyalty. The gift scenes are parallel, and the proverbial commentary applicable to both:

> Then Pippin looked the old man in the eye, for pride stirred strangely within him, still stung by the scorn and suspicion in that cold voice. "Little service, no doubt, will so great a lord of Men think to find in a hobbit, a halfling from the northern Shire; yet such as it is, I will offer it, in payment of my debt." Twitching aside his grey cloak, Pippin drew forth his small sword and laid it at Denethor's feet (III, p. 28).

> "I have a sword," said Merry, climbing from his seat, and drawing from its black sheath his small bright blade. Filled suddenly with love for this old man, he knelt on one knee, and took his hand and kissed it. "May I lay the sword of Meriadoc of the Shire on your lap, Théoden King?" he cried. "Receive my service, if you will" (III, p. 50).

The gift of Merry's loyalty to Théoden is given an initial but unsuccessful check by the old king's own "cold counsel" that he received Merry as his swordthain only for his "safe-keeping," not to fight, for in "such a battle as we think to make on the fields of Gondor what would you do, Master Meriadoc, swordthain though you be, and greater of heart than of stature?" (III, p. 77). But it is of course a good thing for all that despite Théoden's cold counsel and express order, Merry does accompany the Rohirrim to Gondor, for there he does the bravest deed of the day, stabbing the Lord of the Nazgûl with his sword of Westernesse, thereby saving the life of his friend Dernhelm (Éowyn in disguise) and turning the tide of battle.

Éowyn too has rightly refused to let "cold counsel" dis-suade her from journeying to Gondor. Aragorn advises against leaving her duties at Dunharrow and accompanying Rohan to Pelennor. For once he has given way to the demands of intellectually perceived duty rather than to the message of the heart and is thus entirely wrong: "Stay!" he says, "For you have no errand to the South" (III, p. 58). She ignores this cold counsel, and disguising herself as the warrior Dern-helm ("Secret-helmet") she goes herself and carries Merry on her horse, encouraging the hobbit with a proverb that will be basic not only to the plot-line of the minor pair of hobbits, but also, ironically, to Aragorn's subplot as well: *"Where will wants not, a way opens"* (III, p. 77).

The secondary plot-line in Book V again involves two parallels, the twin master strategies of Gandalf and Aragorn to continue fighting and distracting Sauron, keeping his eye ever away from his own land and the hopeless pair creeping toward Orodruin. And again, these subplots are the working out in action of the same two proverbs that stand at the core of meaning behind Merry's and Pippin's roles.

Central to the success of Aragorn's role in the war of Gondor are the positive effects of his great force of will and of his willingness to die, if necessary, on the Paths of the Dead in the hope of getting through to Lebennin and Anduin to stop the Enemy's army advancing on Gondor from the south. That army will beat Rohan to Pelennor and make Gondor's defeat inevitable, unless some way can be found to forestall them, and, as it turns out, only Aragorn can do that. Just before he decides to use the *palantír*, Aragorn receives a providentially timed message from Elrond: "*If thou art in haste, remember the Paths of the Dead*" (III, p. 48). There is no reason, at this point, why he *should* think of that perilous way; he plans simply to accompany Rohan to Gondor. But Elrond has learned from afar something Aragorn will not know until he exerts his will upon the seeing-stone — that a huge army of Haradrim is moving northward up the Anduin. After his contest of will with the Red Eye over the *palantír*, Aragorn is "grey-hued and weary" but has made a decision and a discovery without which the victory on the fields of Pelennor would have been impossible: "I have heard strange words," Aragorn says to Théoden, "and I see new perils far off. I have laboured long in thought, and now I fear that I must change my purpose. Tell me, Théoden, you ride now to Dunharrow, how long will it be ere you come there?" (III, pp. 51–52). On learning it is three days' ride to Dunharrow and yet another week to Gondor, Aragorn realizes he is now indeed in haste and must ride "by the swiftest way . . . the Paths of the Dead" (III, p. 52).

Elrond's message to Aragorn also advises him to remember the "*words of the seer*" — that when "*doom approaches . . . the hour is come for the oathbreakers*" (III, p. 54). Providentially the only quick way to the coastlands and the Haradrim army is likewise the only way to find allies sufficient to conquer that army — the oathbreakers of the Second Age. Furthermore, the power that enabled Aragorn to wrest the seeing-stone from Sauron's control, his force of will ("I spoke no word to him, and in the end I wrenched the Stone to my own will" — III, p. 53), is the only force strong enough to see the travelers through the Paths and to keep the awakened oath-breakers in marching order down to Anduin: "Aragorn led the way, and such was the strength of his will in that hour that all the Dúnedain and their horses followed him" (III, p. 60). And as Legolas says later, "Even the shades of men" were "obedient to his will" (III, p. 151).

Aragorn's use of the *palantír* to reveal himself as King to the eye of the too-long-untroubled Sauron ("To know that I lived and walked the earth was a blow to his heart, I deem," says Aragorn — III, p. 53) will prompt the Enemy's striking more swiftly at Gondor. This knowledge evokes Aragorn's proverb, a saying basic to the two subplots in Book V: "The hasty stroke goes oft astray" (III, p. 54). The same holds true for Gandalf's master strategy in this book; as long as Sauron is seeking to crush Gondor and its newly returned King, he will pay the less attention to Mordor and the hobbits crossing Gorgoroth. And if he can be tricked into thinking that the army approaching Morannon with Aragorn at its head bears the Ring with it, seeking in pride to crush Mordor with a mere seven thousand men, so much the more will his hasty stroke go astray in responding to this threat rather than to the real one. Further, this generous deed, Gandalf's risking all in a desperate last ploy to distract the Eye long enough for Frodo to succeed, is almost checked by "cold counsel" — Prince Imrahil's objection that it is "the greatest jest in all the history of Gondor: that we should ride with seven thousands . . . to assail the mountains and the impenetrable gate of the Black Land" (III, p. 158). But the jest succeeds.

Book VI brings together the two major plot-strands of *The Lord of the Rings* — the adventures of the two pairs of hobbits — presenting the final achievements of each. We recall that the first five books deal with the preliminary adventures of both pairs of hobbits. The first two present in mirror images the initial adventures of the Ringbearer. Book III presents the first set of preliminary adventures of the minor pair, Merry and Pippin. Book IV finds the major pair seeking a way to enter Mordor. The fifth book shifts again to the minor pair, showing them finally attaining full maturity, each saving the life of a great ruler's heir. Book VI presents the major adventure of each pair of hobbits: Frodo and Sam struggling toward Mount Doom to destroy the Ring, Merry and Pippin leading all the hobbits in the scouring of the Shire.

The final adventure of Merry and Pippin has been prepared for by the magical effects of the Entdraught (Law Three), by the objectified force of their own will toward heroism (Law Four), and, most importantly, by the overarching Providence that has "trained" them for their last great work. As Gandalf says, just before the hobbits re-enter the Shire on October 28, "You must settle its affairs yourselves; that is what you have been trained for. Do you not yet understand? My time is over . . . And as for you, my dear friends, you will need no help. You are grown up now. Grown indeed very high" (III, p. 275). This last is in part Gandalf's humorous allusion to the great height of the minor pair, who, under the influence of the Entdraught, are approaching four feet and still growing. By this time, Merry and Pippin have learned the tricks of battle, have earned great courage, and are ready to lead in the scouring of the Shire. And they do lead; Frodo draws no weapon and takes no role in the final cleansing, except to save life whenever possible. His task has been accomplished with the destruction of the Ring, and since March 25 he has been gradually fading, inching toward his departure westward.

In the Frodo-Sam strand of Book VI, three major actions must occur: Frodo must be rescued from the Tower of Cirith Ungol, the major pair must reach Gorgoroth and scale Mount Doom, the Ring must enter the fire.

Escape from the Tower requires the positive and negative sides of the Second Law — the effects of good and bad will. A combination of Orc wickedness and Sam's love for his master gets the major pair safely on the road to Orodruin:

> [Sam] listened; and as he did so a gleam of hope came to him . . . there was fighting in the tower, the Orcs must be at war among themselves . . . Faint as was the hope that his guess brought him, it was enough to rouse him. There might be just a chance. His love for Frodo rose above all other thoughts, and forgetting his peril he cried aloud: "I'm coming, Mr. Frodo" (III, p. 175).

Yet another law is at work in this episode. Sam must first find a way into Cirith Ungol, and he does so in keeping with two physical laws of Middle-earth, the Third (moral and magical law have the force of physical law) and the Fourth (the objective reality of will). Sam at first cannot penetrate the force-field of evil will guarding the entrance to the tower — an unbreakable though invisible wall of malice between the two Watchers. The only power able to break that wall is the elvish magic in the phial of Galadriel, which Sam had faithfully removed from what he believed was the corpse of Frodo. In his moment of need before the Watchers, "because he could think of nothing else to do" (III, p. 179), he holds up the phial, and the barrier of malice evaporates. Sam enters, and the major pair are soon on their way to Gorgoroth.

Frodo and Sam must now cross Mordor to Orodruin in the ten days between March 15 (the date of Frodo's escape) and March 25 (the battle at Morannon) in order to forestall the destruction of the army of the West at the Black Gate (though they know nothing of this heroic ploy on Gandalf's part). But as it happens, the major pair cannot cross Gorgoroth from the west, for the plain is filled solidly from Cirith Ungol to Orodruin with the encamped armies of Sauron. Frodo and Sam must go north, then east, then south, *around* the regiments of Orcs west of Mount Doom — a journey on foot of more than a hundred miles. How, in their weariness, can they do this impossible feat? Their success is the direct result of Gandalf's generously self-sacrificing master strategy, for the hobbits, dressed in Orc clothing, are picked up as stragglers by part of the very army heading north to destroy Gandalf's seven thousand, and force-marched at great speed, covering the fifty miles to Isenmouthe in twenty-four hours, a distance and speed they could never have made on their own without the stimulus of the Orc-captain's whip. As that wicked leader says, "Where there's a whip there's a will"

(III, p. 208), unknowingly expressing Mordor's cruel parody of the proverb basic to both Books V and VI, *"Where will wants not, a way opens"* (III, p. 77).

Middle-earth's laws are fully apparent in the final episodes of the Ring's tale. Utterly exhausted and with weakening will, the hobbits could never have climbed Mount Doom or reached Sammath Naur, but for Sauron's own road to the Chambers of Fire — Tolkien's realization of the proverb "Our Enemy's devices oft serve us in his despite" (III, p. 109). And last of all, the Ring would never have fallen into the fire but for the reversed effects of Gollum's lust for his Precious, satisfied at last, Ringbearer to the Crack of Doom.

THE MYTH ALLEGORIZED

Tolkien's Minor Prose

DESPITE HIS PROTESTATIONS of distaste for the dark conceit ("I cordially dislike allegory in all its manifestations" [I, p. 7]), Tolkien has in fact regarded allegory as a legitimate critical tool — a means to clarify critical stance — throughout his career. As early as the 1936 *Beowulf* lecture, we find him attempting allegory to illustrate what he is about as critic. *Beowulf* had been dealt with by almost everyone except critics, he declared, and he wanted the situation remedied:

> A sketch of the history of the subject is required. But I will here only attempt, for brevity's sake, to present my view of it allegorically. As it set out upon its adventures among the modern scholars, *Beowulf* was christened by Wanley Poesis — *Poeseos Anglo-Saxonicae egregium exemplum.* But the fairy godmother later invited to superintend its fortunes was Historia. And she brought with her Philologia, Mythologia, Archaeologia, and Laographia. Excellent Ladies. But where was the child's namesake? Poesis was usually forgotten; occasionally admitted by a side-door; sometimes dismissed upon the door-step.[1]

At least two other times in his career, and both times at some length, Tolkien has turned to allegory to make what were for him deeply important personal statements about fantasy. Both "Leaf by Niggle" (written 1938-1939, published 1947) and "Smith of Wootton Major" (published 1967, though perhaps written some years earlier[2]) are allegorical statements about the tremendous power of the "spell of *Faërie*" in Tolkien's life and about his own joys and fears at entering and writing of the Perilous Realm.

The earlier of these works is closely connected with the essay "On Fairy-Stories"; in fact, it says very much the same things in narrative terms that the essay says in discursive. "Leaf by Niggle" is a charming piece of therapeutic allegory that belongs with the essay both chronologically and functionally, as Tolkien admitted when he republished both works in 1964 under the one title *Tree and Leaf*. They were, he writes, products of a winter of imaginative discontent in 1938-1939, when he was beginning "to despair of surviving" to complete *The Lord of the Rings*. At that time his masterpiece "was beginning to unroll itself and to unfold prospects of labour and exploration in yet unknown country."[3] He had written the first half of Book I ("we had reached Bree") when he seemed to suffer a momentary imaginative inhibition, a despairing suspicion that to continue his gigantic work of fantasy was pointless and vain. A brief passage in the "Fairy-Stories" essay gives us an apt description of how he probably felt in the winter of 1938-1939, and in words that reveal the origin of the central symbol in "Leaf by Niggle" — the tree: "It is easy," he writes of the author of a fairy story, "to feel that with all his labour he is collecting only a few leaves, many of them now torn or decayed, from the countless foliage of the Tree of Tales, with which the Forest of Days is carpeted. It seems vain to add to the litter. Who can design a new leaf?" (TL, p. 56). Who indeed? he probably asked himself, bogged down in Bree with seemingly nowhere to go. Feeling thus, in that winter, Tolkien observed one day that a poplar tree in view of his bedroom window had been "lopped and mutilated by its owner" for no apparent reason. Here was a suddenly meaningful symbol for his fear of his own death, his "despair of surviving" to find out the end of *The Lord of the Rings*, a despair resulting from his continued inability fully to grasp the role and function of Faërie, that "unknown country as daunting to me as to the hobbits." So the poplar tree became "one of [the] sources" of "Leaf" and its lopping a sudden catalyst for the necessary internal reaction, the imaginative grasp of the meaning of fantasy creation, for release came soon after the mutilation, by an unconscious process of internal solution, when, as Tolkien says, the story "reached manuscript form, very swiftly, one day when I awoke with it already in mind" (TL, pp. vii–viii). Work began again on *The Lord of the Rings*.

Tolkien's imagination-deadening fear he would not survive to design his own leaf is transmuted into an allegory about a niggling self-portrait of the artist — Niggle by name —whose creating does not stop when he dies. "Leaf by Niggle" is Tolkien's imagination's promise to itself that no genuine creation ever ceases to be, that the best of one's imaginings permanently enriches reality. "There was once a little man called Niggle, who had a long journey to make. He did not want to go, indeed the whole idea was distasteful to him; but he could not get out of it" (TL, p. 87). How closely Tolkien's imagination has identified itself with its hobbit creations! The quest pattern is present even in his dreams, for Bilbo and Frodo, too, have long journeys to make that they do not want to begin, but cannot avoid. Niggle's journey is of course his own death, the symbolic product of Tolkien's depressed fears in 1938-1939.

"Niggle was a painter. Not a very successful one, partly because he had many other things to do. Most of these things he thought were a nuisance; but he did them fairly well, when he could not get out of them: which (in his opinion) was far too often" (TL, p. 87). The humility in the self-portrait ("a little man, . . . not . . . very successful") is apparently necessary to Tolkien's own complex internal readjustment effected in the story. At any rate, the self-portrait is accurate. Niggle's lack of success as a painter because of his "other things," never really finishing his great work, reminds us of Tolkien's own situation during the creation of *The Lord of the Rings,* which took, he has written in its Foreword, "a long time; for the composition . . . went on at intervals during the years 1936 to 1949, a period in which I had many duties that I did not neglect, and many other interests as a learner and teacher that often absorbed me" (I, p. 5). Those duties were transmuted, in the belittling self-appraisal of the allegory (as the artist part of himself speaks, in opposition to the public, professional part) into the nuisance activities he could not avoid.

The question of the would-be artist's responsibility toward his community is a key theme in "Leaf by Niggle," presented in the relationship between Niggle and his neighbor Parish. The artist's community is his "parish" — already we begin to grasp Tolkien's notion of art's contribution to society; just as the parish centers and depends on its church and vicar for spiritual guidance and relevant insight, so Parish depends on Niggle, not only for neighborly support — every neighbor must give that — but finally, for vision itself. Niggle, Tolkien remarks of himself, "was kindhearted, in a way. You know the sort of kind heart: it made him uncomfortable more often than it made him do anything; and even when he did anything, it did not prevent him from grumbling, losing his temper, and swearing (mostly to himself). All the same, it did land him in a good many odd jobs for his neighbour, Mr. Parish, a man with a lame leg" (TL, p. 87). The artist's community is marred and requires continual aid. A former Oxford student has told me in conversation that once he and some friends were sitting together and puzzling over the medieval poem *The Owl and the Nightingale* when Tolkien (who was not their tutor) approached and asked what was the matter. The upshot was that he spent the rest of the afternoon with them working through the difficulties of the poem — a free and typical gift of his limited time. Doubtless within himself the part that kept him up nights writing *The Lord of the Rings* was loudly protesting (with curses) this "nuisance," but, as he wrote of Niggle, "The laws in his country were rather strict," and one of Tolkien's laws was devotion to students, even those not his own — just as Niggle too "helped other people from further off, if they came and asked him" (TL, p. 87).

Like Tolkien, Niggle the artist had started a small work, a work of joy in minute labors, that had somehow got out of hand:

> There was one picture in particular which bothered him. It had begun with a leaf caught in the wind, and it became a tree; and the tree grew, sending out innumerable branches, and thrusting out the most fantastic roots. Strange birds came and settled on the twigs and had to be attended to. Then all round the Tree, and behind it, through the gaps

in the leaves and boughs, a country began to open
out; and there were glimpses of a forest marching
over the land, and of mountains tipped with snow
(TL, p. 88).

Here is a clear allegorical description of the inexorable and
well-nigh overwhelming growth, in Tolkien's mind, of *The
Hobbit*'s leaf into the great world of *The Lord of the Rings*.
Niggle's exasperation and delight at his great and apparently
unfinishable picture is precisely Tolkien's feeling about his
work in progress in 1938, a work out of which is growing
a country altogether "daunting" to its author. Niggle's pride
is Tolkien's as well: it "seemed to him . . . the only really
beautiful picture in the world" (TL, p. 89); Tolkien once
remarked that the only fault of the *Rings* is that it is "too
short" (I, p. 6).

Like Tolkien, Niggle is unable to work full-time on his
art because of constant interruptions from people with legitimate claims on his time but who fail utterly to grasp the
importance of his private work. "When Parish looked at
Niggle's garden [his "real" work] . . . he saw mostly weeds;
and when he looked at Niggle's pictures (which was seldom)
he saw only green and grey patches and black lines, which
seemed to him nonsensical" (TL, p. 91). (Imagine what a
member of the British Academy, who regarded even the
dragon in *Beowulf* as a piece of nonsense, would have said
about *The Lord of the Rings*!)

Like Tolkien's students, Parish comes asking help; his wife
is ill with fever, and he cannot, with his lame leg, fetch the
doctor. So Niggle, boiling inwardly ("his fingers twitched
on the handlebars" [TL, p. 93]), leaves his picture and goes
on his bicycle in the rain, catches a chill, and takes to his
bed for a week. The day after he gets up, a very tall man

dressed all in black enters Niggle's house and says, "Come along! . . . You start today on your journey, you know" (TL, pp. 95–96). Niggle's act of charity has given him his death of a cold. At this point begins, in earnest, Tolkien's profoundly perceptive allegorical study of the spiritual functions of art and the role of the artist in fulfilling them.

Since his counterpart is a Roman Catholic, the dead Niggle naturally proceeds to purgatory, though Tolkien never names it as such. Like Everyman, Niggle enters the underworld with nothing, not even baggage, so with the poorest of the dead, he must go "to the Workhouse." Fainting at this doleful news, he is carried to the Workhouse Infirmary — a purgatory that will burn off his earthly faults and leave him with only his artistic skills and soul's purity:

> He did not like the treatment at all. The medicine they gave him was bitter. The officials and attendants were unfriendly, silent, and strict . . . It was more like being in a prison than in a hospital. He had to work hard, at stated hours: at digging, carpentry, and painting bare boards all one plain colour (TL, p. 97).

The artist's pride is purged in performing the meanest crafts, and Niggle takes to the treatment well, beginning soon to repent his misdeeds: "I wish I had called on Parish the first morning after the high winds began . . . Then Mrs. Parish might never have caught cold" (TL, p. 97).

Niggle progresses rapidly, in the purgatorial time scale. After "the first century or so" (TL, p. 97), he can work as never before, taking "up a task the moment one bell rang, [laying] it aside promptly the moment the next one went . . . He got through quite a lot in a day, now." He even

stops cursing, as he gradually gets " 'better' by some odd
medical standard" (TL, p. 98) of the place: his soul's state.
His hardest lesson, the one he is slowest to grasp (and the
one Tolkien needs desperately to believe so that he can return
with vigor to Frodo at Bree) is that the value of an artist's
skill and accomplishment is inseparable from his relationship
with his community. Niggle at last realizes that "the most
characteristic, the most perfect examples of the Niggle style
— were . . . produced in collaboration with Mr. Parish: there
was no other way of putting it" (TL, p. 104). Thus comes
Niggle's last lesson at the Workhouse: the artist's proper
concern for his community. When told he is finally ready
for "gentle treatment," he can only ask, in reply, "Could
you tell me about Parish?" (TL, p. 101), proving that he has
indeed earned entry to the next stage of purgatory.

Traveling there, appropriately on the bicycle used in his
last charitable act, Niggle begins to recognize the terrain,
to remember having "seen or dreamed" it sometime, and
then suddenly, like Saul on the road to Damascus, "Niggle
looked up, and fell off his bicycle. Before him stood the
Tree, his Tree, finished" (TL, p. 103). The Tree is complete,
but not the surrounding forest: "there were a number of
inconclusive regions, that still needed work and thought."
Yet despite seeing what he needs to do, "He could not quite
work out his scheme," because as artist, he is incomplete,
impotent, without the presence of the other element in
sub-creative activity — his community. "Of course!" he said.
"What I need is Parish. There are lots of things about earth,
plants, and trees that he knows and I don't. This place cannot
be left just as my private park. I need help and advice"
(TL, pp. 105–106). So Parish appears, released from his own
Workhouse ("Thank you for putting in a word for me," he

tells his friend. "It got me out a lot sooner"). They set to work: "Niggle would think of wonderful new flowers and plants, and Parish always knew exactly how to set them and where they would do best . . . Parish lost his limp" (TL, pp. 106–107). The artist creates, the community disposes and benefits; Tolkien has imaginatively answered one of the problems that had vexed him since departing from Middle-earth. He has resolved the internal dilemma of the conflicting pulls on the time of the professor who wants to write; "Leaf by Niggle" is the imaginative solution.

At length, "Niggle's country" is complete and the artist looks toward the next stage; like Christian in *Pilgrim's Progress*, he begins to yearn for the Delectable Mountains lying on the unexplored edges of his picture: Niggle is at last ready for heaven. Parish elects to wait for his wife, who had, it seems, more time to spend in the Workhouse. With Niggle's job finished and the artist's task understood, Tolkien gives himself, at the very end, the best of all justifications for *The Lord of the Rings* and ample reason to want to return and finish his own "country." The Second Voice, who mercifully released Niggle from the Workhouse, explains the present uses of the completed picture (now called Niggle's Parish): "It is proving very useful indeed . . . As a holiday, and a refreshment. It is splendid for convalescence; and not only for that, for many it is the best introduction to the Mountains. It works wonders in some cases. I am sending more and more there. They seldom have to come back" (TL, p. 112).

This last paragraph was Tolkien's final inhibition-remover. Bree was waiting, as soon as he could tell himself these things — the same things, really, that he had already said in "On Fairy-Stories" but in a form more convincing to the imagination: that the realm of the artist's fantasy is in fact the realm of his spirit, that his moral and aesthetic relation to his audience is a portion of his own soul's state, that creation is in fact a necessary collaboration between artist and community, and that it does the one as much good as the other. He needed to tell himself in narrative, not just discursive terms, that the cosmos is friendly to sub-creation, because it echoes its own chief and most joyous activity, that like Niggle's Mountains, heaven lies at the farthest boundary of each successful Secondary World, that participation in an act of sub-creation is in fact preparation for spiritual experience, that the pleasures of Faërie are at their purest indistinguishable from spiritual joy, and, finally, that fantasy can bear the Good News, in its minor way, even in the company of the evangelists themselves.

9

Like "Leaf by Niggle," "Smith of Wootton Major" is not strictly a work of Faërie. True fantasy, according to Tolkien's own rule, takes place *inside* Faërie; there is no going to and from, no framing device set in the Primary World, nor is there allegory. Yet "Smith" and "Leaf" have both — a Primary-World "frame" at beginning and end, and a closely worked allegory. In both works Tolkien is presenting a message, not a work of Faërie; true fantasy is nought but pure narrative, potent enough in the telling only and requiring no overlay of "meaning." Tolkien uses other devices to have his say *about* Faërie, and it seems that allegory is for him a favorite.

I have a suspicion that when Tolkien's final work, *The Silmarillion,* appears, we shall find that "Smith" bears an allegorical relationship toward this work analogous to that between "Leaf by Niggle" and *The Lord of the Rings*. As "Leaf" is Tolkien's allegorical account of his discovery of the richness and function of Faërie, "Smith" is his early farewell to that Perilous Realm, another allegory in which he is again the central figure. The story tells, through the person and adventures of Smith, what it means to have the gift of Faërie, the right to enter a Secondary World at will and bring back wonders of elvish craft, beauties to ease the burdened hearts of men, and what it means, after long years, to give it up, pass it on, and prepare to die.

"Smith," again like "Leaf by Niggle," is cast in a narrative pattern deeply related to the pattern we have found in Tolkien's nonallegorical explorations of Faërie. Just as Niggle must, like Bilbo and Frodo, go on a journey he dreads, so the Master Cook of Wootton Major goes off one day to everyone's surprise, only to come back from Faërie a few months later, deeply changed, filled, like Bilbo, with the elvish wonders he has seen. Just as Bilbo turns to writing poetry after visiting Rivendell, and brings back with him a marvelous and mysterious work of Faëriean craft, the Ring, so Master Cook "came back some months later [and] seemed rather changed . . . Now he was merrier, and often said and did most laughable things; and at feasts he would himself sing gay songs, which was not expected of Master Cooks. Also he brought back with him an Apprentice," named Alf.[4] With this, Tolkien is telling us something, for "Alf" is the Old Norse word for "Elf"; indeed, we later learn, Alf is no less than the King of Faërie.

Again, like Bilbo, the Master Cook goes off on a *second* journey late in his life, leaving the magical object he had earned on his first trip to Faërie in the hands of his successor. Cook says to Alf, "Tell them I've gone on another holiday"

(p. 9), just as Bilbo says to Gandalf, before his second journey to Rivendell, "I need a holiday" (I, p. 40). Both leave for Faërie, causing no small stir and wonderment in their towns: "What a thing to do!" they said in Wootton (p. 9), while the talk of Bilbo's disappearance from Hobbiton "did not die down in nine or even ninety-nine days" (I, p. 51).

The people of Wootton Major, not recognizing the King of Faery (as Tolkien calls it in this story) in the person of Alf the Prentice, choose instead for the next Master Cook a barely honest and heavily unimaginative plodder named Nokes, who usually manages to "trick" the knowing Alf into doing the Master Cook's more difficult tasks. We learn later in the story that Alf has come on purpose to Wootton from Faery in order to oversee the passing on of a fay star kept in a spice box in the kitchen of the Great Hall. The singing and traveling Master Cook of past notoriety (Smith's grandfather, in fact) had held it during his time — using it for the gift of entering Faery that it conveyed and undergoing the changes Faery brings — and then had gone off, leaving it to be passed to his grandson.

Nokes takes over, and his one memorable task will be the preparation of the Great Cake, baked but once every twenty-four years for The Feast of Good Children. He dreams up a rather vulgar sugar-iced concoction, with a doll tippy-toeing on its pinnacle as the Fairy Queen, and gives Alf the job of making the frosting. Smith, aged nine, is invited, the star is baked in the cake, and he swallows it, as Alf has planned.

With the effects of the star on Smith begins Tolkien's central statement about the powers of beauty: the gift of the right to enter Faërie comes but once in a generation or so, but it is bestowed by the King himself (i.e., the gift of writing genuine fairy stories is rare indeed, a gift from God). The chief value of the gift (Tolkien's pun is intentional) is the ability to perceive and create beauty, which in turn brings positive moral good (true, Tolkien hopes, of his own gift of Secondary Creation). The result of the gift in Smith is that his voice began "to grow beautiful as soon as the star came to him, [and] became ever more beautiful as he grew up" (p. 20). He takes up his father's trade of blacksmithing and makes things of great and healing beauty:

> Most of them, of course, were plain and useful, meant for daily needs: farm tools, carpenters' tools, kitchen tools . . . They were strong and lasting, but they also had a grace about them, being shapely in their kinds, good to handle and to look at.
> But some things, when he had time, he made for delight; and they were beautiful, for he could work iron into wonderful forms that looked as light and delicate as a spray of leaves and blossom, but kept the stern strength of iron, or seemed even stronger . . . He sang when he was making things of this sort; and when Smith began to sing those nearby stopped their own work and came to the smithy to listen (p. 21).

Smith also uses his right to enter Faery, going frequently to the Perilous Realm for its many secrets. Tolkien's narrative of Smith's adventures in Faery is a brief allegorical history of his own experiences in that realm during the creation of *The Hobbit* and the *Rings*. With *The Hobbit*, as Tolkien later implicitly admitted in "On Fairy-Stories," he had entered Faërie in the wrong spirit, with the wrong understanding of its true purpose and audience. The discovery of his mistake dismayed Tolkien, but he was nonetheless captured heart and soul by his Secondary World and could not leave it alone. At his darkest moment, when he was both irrevocably enchanted by his Middle-earth and yet unable to move any farther into it, a tree, lopped and stripped bare, appeared to him as a symbol of his state with regard to Faërie, and its mutilation was a bitter thing to him. But release came through the symbols of tree and leaf (i.e., the writing of "On Fairy-Stories" and "Leaf by Niggle") and he resolved to continue. He re-entered Middle-earth, this time with success, going right to the heart of Faërie, and completed *The Lord of the Rings.* We find the same story, in allegorical form, in Tolkien's account of Smith.

Like Tolkien, Smith in the beginning relates his experiences in Faery only to his wife and children. And "In Faery at first he walked for the most part quietly among the lesser folk and the gentler creatures in the woods and meads of fair valleys . . . Some of his briefer visits he spent looking only at one tree or one flower" (pp. 24-26) — just as Tolkien at first makes only the leaf called *The Hobbit,* which touches but lightly on the real beauty and terror of Faërie. Indeed it is only "later in longer journeys" that Smith sees "things of both beauty and terror" (p. 26), just as Tolkien only later, in *The Lord of the Rings,* realizes like Smith that "the marvels of Faery cannot be approached without danger" (p. 24). Tolkien himself does not explicitly state that the realm of Faërie is perilous until after the completion of *The Hobbit,* when, in writing "On Fairy-Stories," he tried to work out what his children's story had taught him. There he said that "Faërie is a perilous land, and in it are pitfalls for the unwary and dungeons for the overbold. And overbold I may be accounted" (TL, p. 3). Just as Tolkien with overboldness undertook too lightly the perilous entry into Faërie with *The Hobbit*, Smith imagines too lightly that "without a guide . . . he would discover the further bounds of the land" (p. 26). But Smith learns to his pain that no one discovers without labor and thought, and peril to himself, the secrets of Faery. Traveling around the outer mountains of that realm, Smith comes to the Sea of Windless Storm and finds things that leave "his heart . . . shaken with fear" (p. 26). Moving inland, he encounters the same symbols of tree and leaf so important to Tolkien. Smith finds the King's Tree, symbol of all Faëriean invention, that "bore at once leaves and flowers and fruits uncounted" (p. 28). Further inland, he discovers a lake of pure crystal, and slips on its glassy surface:

> At once the breeze rose to a wild Wind, roaring like a great beast, and it swept him up and . . . drove him up the slopes whirling and falling like a dead leaf. He put his arms about the stem of a young birch and clung to it, and the Wind wrestled fiercely with them, trying to tear him away; but the birch was bent down to the ground by the blast and enclosed him in its branches. When at last the Wind passed on he rose and saw that the birch was naked. It was stripped of every leaf, and it wept (p. 29).

Here is a clear allegorical picture of Tolkien's own reaction to the turmoil caused in him by his too lightly entering Faërie and then "slipping," early in *The Lord of the Rings*, into momentary imaginative inhibition, but being released by a leafless tree. Tolkien might well echo Smith's words, "Blessed be the birch" (p. 30) — though of course *his* tree was a poplar. Smith's reaction to this incident is very like Tolkien's own inability in 1938 to proceed into Middle-earth:

"His heart was saddened, . . . and for some time he did not enter Faery again. But he could not forsake it, and when he returned his desire was still stronger to go deep into the land" (p. 30). Smith goes right to the heart of Faery, dancing in the Vale of Evermorn with the very Queen of that land and later receiving a message for the King himself: *"The time has come. Let him choose"* (p. 38). The message means, as Smith learns later, that it is time for him to give up the star, pass on the gift of Faery, though he will have the right to choose its recipient. Here we move back into the moral heart of Tolkien's own exploration of Faërie, *The Lord of the Rings*, for "Smith" shares a central theme with that work: a good man has received from a relative a great gift, of incalculable Faëriean power, and must give it up. Smith's dilemma parallels both Bilbo's and Frodo's, and the scene of Smith's hard decision willingly to give up the star closely parallels Bilbo's hard-fought choice to pass the Ring on to Frodo. Bilbo has grown old, and like Smith's grandfather, needs a "holiday." But Gandalf tells him that before he goes, he had best give up the Ring: " 'I think, Bilbo,' he said quietly, 'I should leave it behind.' " Bilbo grows angry and suspicious: "I don't really see why I should . . . And what business is it of yours, anyway, to know what I do with my own things? It is my own. I found it. It came to me" (I, pp. 41–42). Smith echoes Bilbo's very words when Alf says, " 'Do you not think, Master Smith,. . . that it is time for you to give this thing up?' 'What is that to you, Master Cook,' he answered. 'And why should I do so? Isn't it mine? It came to me' " (p. 41). In other words Smith's star and Bilbo's Ring are deeply related in Tolkien's imagination. Both are symbols to him of the power of Faërie, the Perilous Realm which at age seventy-two in 1967 he had been exploring for thirty years — and like Smith he is loath to give up the joy of going to and from that beautiful place. Yet he knows it will be but a few years at most before that tall man dressed all in black comes to him as to Niggle saying, "Come along! . . . You start today on your journey." Smith's and Niggle's unwillingness is Tolkien's own, and telling of it, easing the burden in story, makes the hard end gentler.

LAST GLEANINGS
FROM THE RED BOOK
Scholarly Parody in
The Adventures of Tom Bombadil

TOLKIEN IS not only the historian, geographer, ethnographer, and philologist of his world of Middle-earth but its literary executor as well. Six years after the publication of *The Return of the King,* he announced that the Red Book of Westmarch, the mythical red-leather-bound volume from which earlier he had soberly declared he faithfully copied the accounts of Bilbo's and Frodo's adventures, also "contains a large number of verses."[1] Then in an exquisite parody of a scholarly introduction to a long-lost manuscript, he proceeded to describe the Red Book and its newly deciphered contents, and solemnly to theorize about their authorship, sources, and linguistic relationships. Thus begins one of the best jokes in recent literary history, for not only does the preface parody the methods of textual and philological scholarship, but many of the poems in the little volume *The Adventures of Tom Bombadil* are parodies and final "solutions" to notorious scholarly hobbyhorses of Tolkien's time. With loving humor, he gently deflates some of the more puffy parts of two things dear to him, his hobbit creations and his profession of literary and philological scholarship.

Tolkien has always looked with a twinkle in his eye at the vagaries and pitfalls of scholarship in his special field of Old English literature; he once quoted with glee Oswald Cockayne's conviction that Tolkien's nineteenth-century predecessor in the Rawlinson Chair of Anglo-Saxon at Oxford, Joseph Bosworth, had not read all the books "printed in our old English, or so-called Anglosaxon tongue. He may do very well for a professor."[2] The twinkle enlarges into delicious laughter in *The Adventures of Tom Bombadil.*

Like Tolkien's more important imaginative works, this little volume grows from a matrix of professional interests and activities. As a scholar of Medieval British literature, he studied two ancient collections of Welsh bardic poetry, the Black Book of Carmarthen and the Red Book of Hergest (he cites the first in the notes to his edition of *Sir Gawain and the Green Knight*). Sadly, only students of Welsh culture know these great collections, largely because of the weak scholarship and worse translations in the standard English version, *The Four Ancient Books of Wales,* edited by William F. Skene. Tolkien modeled his own Red Book after the Welsh volume, partly, it would seem, as a parody of Skene's poor work. This aspect of Tolkien's joke began some twenty years before the *Bombadil* volume, in the "Note on the Shire Records" prefacing *The Fellowship of the Ring,* where he seems to allude to Skene in his explanation of the name of the Red Book of Westmarch ("so called because it was long preserved at Undertowers, the home of the Fairbairns, Wardens of the Westmarch" — I, p. 23). A century before, Skene had declared that "The Red Book of Hergest is said to have been so termed from its having been compiled for the Vaughans of Hergest Court, Herefordshire."[3] But the "Note on the Shire Records" is really not intended as a joke, it is part of the deadly serious business of establishing Secondary Belief. The conventional fantasy device of the "discovered manuscript" works here in a quietly insistent way to "convince" the reader of the reality and history of Middle-earth. But Tolkien's sense of humor about his profession being what it was, he finally could not resist the temptation to exploit the possibilities for satire latent in the discovered-manuscript convention. Indeed, the idea seems not to have come to him until *after* the "Note" to *The Fellowship*, for that Note mentions no marginal verses in the Red Book.

There are two separate kinds of joke in *The Adventures of Tom Bombadil*, one the scholarly parody already mentioned, the other stemming from Tolkien's amused affection for his hobbit creations. This second element of humor begins in the preface to the volume with Tolkien's soberly maintained fiction that not he but a group of mostly nameless rustic hobbits wrote the poems, which are for the most part humorous doggerel. This neat but simple ploy opens some lovely comic possibilities. On the simplest level there is self-parody; the more transparent the device for "protecting" the poems from the charge of being simply Tolkien's bad verse, the more fun the realization that this is indeed what most of them are. Tolkien can thus be both hidden poet and amused critic at once, can have the fun of constructing the jingly doggerel of the Shire and the equal fun of assuming the stance of the critic superior to all this, explaining that hobbits were "fond of strange words, and of rhyming and metrical tricks — in their simplicity Hobbits evidently regarded such things as virtues or graces" — an ironic criticism delightfully undercut by the subsequent comment: "though they were, no doubt, mere imitations of Elvish practices" (TB, p. 9). Further, as poems by hobbits, rather than by

Tolkien, they assume a genuinely transforming context, becoming richly descriptive of Tolkien's world and its inhabitants, constituting in fact a poetic critique of the various levels of aesthetic achievement in Middle-earth. In "discovering" the poetry of the Shire, a little world of the past with its own social classes and subliteratures, Tolkien allows us to peer into the creative minds of "Bilbo," "Sam Gamgee," "unnamed hobbit scribblers," and other mute inglorious Miltons of the Third Age, and to observe that some of them — Bilbo especially — were blessed with a remarkably sensitive ear and a real gift for narrative invention, while others suffered the twin ill fates of tin ears and imaginative poverty. Even more clearly than in *The Lord of the Rings,* with its richly comic scenes at *The Green Dragon* and *The Ivy Bush* in Bywater, reminiscent of George Eliot's lovingly presented peasant exchanges, we see through these poems into the rustic mind of the Shire, into its rich though homely sense of humor and its typically hobbitean love of ancient tales, mythic beast-lore, and cracker-barrel wisdom. *The Adventures of Tom Bombadil* evokes an image of the inner mind of the Shire in a way no narrative or essay ever could and thus gives an even deeper life to the little world depicted in *The Lord of the Rings.* Admittedly no one yet uncaptured by the enchantment of Tolkien's world will find much pleasure in these poems, dependent as they are on prior knowledge of Middle-earth, but then Tolkien is not addressing such a person in the verses or the preface anyway.

The sixteen poems of *The Adventures of Tom Bombadil* range from the graceless doggerel of Numbers one and two, the title poem and "Bombadil goes Boating," to the witty beast-lore of ten, eleven, and twelve, "Oliphaunt," "Fastitocalon," and "Cat," to the delicious froth of three, the best of the group and a stunningly skillful piece of versification, "Errantry." Indeed if it were not for the smooth and lovely rhythms of the last, we might be justified on the basis of Numbers one and two of judging that Tolkien is a painfully unskilled poet, worthy of none but derisive attention. Yet knowledge of a piece like Number three puts them into a new light, transforming their roughness to a sign of a certain skill, necessary to contrive such agonies of rhythmic and syntactic wrenching. Here blossoms the Halfling wit; not "Tolkien," but certain unnamed hobbits of Buckland "wrote" these poems. The philologist and geographer of Middle-earth assures us they are "Bucklandish," for the name "Bombadil," he says, betrays that dialect of the Westron tongue spoken by the rustic hobbits beyond the Brandywine; moreover, the poems "evidently come from the Buckland" itself, for they show close "knowledge of that country, and of the Dingle, the wooded valley of the Withywindle" (TB, pp. 8–9). Tolkien then proceeds, in a deliciously mock scholarly footnote, to place and describe the Middle-earthly locations mentioned in one and two and to give the derivations of the place names from the Bucklandish dialect: *"Grindwall"* (a small hythe protected by a *grind* or fence extending down into the water), *"Breredon"* (Briar Hill, a little village on rising ground behind the hythe), and the *"Mithe"* (the mouth of a small stream called the Shirebourn, from which a lane ran to Deephollow and so on to the Causeway) (TB, p. 9).

Ascription of the graceless narrative of Number two (a lumpish account of Tom's Withywindle journey to Farmer Maggot's wet carouse) to the inhabitants of the most rustic and outlying area of hobbitdom is a keen stroke on Tolkien's part, a final justification for its (deliberately) rough texture and rude sense of fun. And rude it is: on the way down the river, Tom encounters a scolding kingfisher and jokingly threatens to pull off his beak and hang it on a string for a weather vane. On being splashed by a river otter, he tries to brain the creature with an oar and threatens to give its hide to the Barrow-wights. All this is in fun, of course, but the nature of the fun exhibits a certain coarseness in the "writers," the rough farmers of Buckland.

A similar coarseness of humor prevails in Number one, which tells of Bombadil's meeting and winning of Goldberry, and of his outwitting Old Man Willow and an unfriendly family of badgers. With rough peasant humor, the poem tells of Goldberry's wooing of Tom by pulling him bodily into the Withywindle, and of his winning of the River-woman's daughter by simply grabbing her and carrying her home with the shrewd advice that she would certainly find no lover in the river. And the meter is as rough as the humor. A strongly galumphing collection of trochaic couplets, the poem exhibits a rustic hobbit's real difficulty in mastering his metrical form; often it abandons its singsong suddenly to find itself the merest rhymed prose, as in the twelfth stanza:

> Out came Badger-brock with his snowy forehead
> and his dark blinking eyes. In the hill he quarried
> with his wife and many sons. By the coat they caught him,
> pulled him inside their earth, down their tunnels brought him.

The first line manages to stick fairly close to the metrical norm, but lines two and three totally lose control until after the caesura in three, when our hobbit poet with a valiant effort hauls himself back into trochees.

Tolkien's implicit commentary on the somehow lovable intellectual shortcomings of his hobbit creations continues in many of the poems. Just as Numbers one and two "show that the Bucklanders knew Bombadil, though, no doubt, they had as little understanding of his powers as the Shire-folk had of Gandalf's" (TB, p. 9), as Tolkien says in his preface, so do poems like four, fourteen, fifteen, and sixteen show that even though the hobbits of the Shire scribbled into the Red Book margins poems about elves, gold-lust, journeys to an unknown land, and passage into the west, their understanding of these things was most inadequate. The humor of these poems lies, at least in part, in our recognition of the limitations of their authors' grasp of what they wrote about. Perhaps the clearest example of this sort of joke is to be found in Number four, "Princess Mee."

Tolkien never tired of fulminating against the vulgar misconception of elves as twinkly-toe'd Little People, dancing around the toadstools; indeed he devoted a whole section of "On Fairy-Stories" to tracing some possible origins of the notion (and found both Shakespeare and Michael Drayton guilty of furthering it). Having attacked the vulgar error, however, he feels free to commit it himself, in such poems as Number three, "Errantry," and Number four, "Princess Mee." Again, though, the joke of the discovered manuscript is at work, and Tolkien would simply reply to the charge of vulgarizing elves in these poems with a reminder that he, after all, did not write them but is merely their editor. We can, then, delightfully enjoy the double gift of joining Tolkien in chuckling at his own amusing doggerel, and of observing the less-than-keen poetic mind of the Shire at work as it fantasizes on the elves about whom it has for the most part only heard fireside tales. "Princess Mee," for example, lets us see how the mind of the Shire wants very much to know about elves and their doings, but feels more comfortable hearing about the kind of elves who dance on water at night under the stars than about masters of power and knowledge like Elrond.

Number four tells about a lovely elf princess with "gossamer" kerchief, "moth-web" coat, and "slippers frail/Of fishes' mail," who spends her evenings pirouetting on the surface of her "dancing-pool." But the poem is more than a parody of too-cute notions of elves, it is also a deliberately contrived tissue of logical flaws of the sort that would make an old-fashioned critic throw up his hands in despair. Princess Mee, for example, walks regularly at night to her dancing-pool "And on mirror cool/Of windless water played." But despite the fact that the syntax of the poem insists that she goes there *nightly*, the whole point of the story is that on one particular evening, apparently for the first time, Princess Mee notices, directly beneath her feet, her reflection: "A Princess Shee/ As fair as Mee." The expected conclusion exploits Mee's puzzlement at Shee's "strange . . . Hanging" upside-down beneath her, and at the fact that "Only their feet/ Could ever meet." The poem clearly has value only as a humorous depiction of the minds of its nameless hobbit authors and admirers.

As we move closer to the center of the Shire, to Hobbiton, we gradually ascend its social and intellectual ladder, though never, of course, to elvish heights. There were few hobbits in the Shire who attended to other than their farms and trades, but those who did sometimes made an effort to learn Elvish and some of its rich oral literature. One of these was Bilbo Baggins, whose stories of elves and their bewitchingly lovely songs set afire the mind of young Samwise Gamgee, the Bagginses' gardener. "Mr. Bilbo has learned him his letters," Sam's father Hamfast proudly tells his friends at *The Ivy Bush*, and "he listens to all Mr. Bilbo's tales" (I, p. 32). Moved by Bilbo's teaching and tales to some composition of his own, Sam made a poem that has the same rough peasant humor as the first two, but clearly surpasses them in metrical and narrative skill. Bilbo's Elvish-inspired influence did much for the young Sam and was of course his initial preparation to be Frodo's companion on the Quest. Indeed, on one quiet evening during Frodo's journey to Rivendell in Book I, Sam recites the poem (I, pp. 219–20) that apparently gained some fame in the Shire, finding its way into the collection of verses that certain anonymous hobbits scribbled into the pages of the Red Book. The poem, "The Stone Troll," is an excellent and very witty piece of doggerel, with a skillfully contrived refrain and a fine comic moral — never kick a stone-troll's behind, for you'll break your foot.

Tom finds a troll gnawing an old bone, and is shocked to discover that it "looks like the shin o' my nuncle Tim/ As should be a-lyin' in graveyard."

> Said Tom: "I don't see why the likes o' thee
> Without axin' leave should go makin' free
>   With the shank or the shin o' my father's kin;
>   So hand the old bone over!
>   Rover! Trover!
>   Though dead he be, it belongs to he;
>   So hand the old bone over!"
>
> "For a couple o' pins," says Troll, and grins,
> "I'll eat thee too, and gnaw thy shins.
>   A bit o' fresh meat will go down sweet!
>   I'll try my teeth on thee now.
>   Hee now! See now!
>   I'm tired o' gnawing old bones and skins;
>   I've a mind to dine on thee now."

Troll lunges, Tom ducks and whirls, and delivers a swift kick.

But harder than stone is the flesh and bone
Of a troll that sits in the hills alone.
As well set your foot to the mountain's root,
For the seat of a troll don't feel it.
Peel it! Heal it!
Old Troll laughed, when he heard Tom groan,
And he knew his toes could feel it.

We are, with "The Stone-Troll," clearly a long way from poetry but still a little closer than with "Bombadil goes Boating." The other verses in the collection that are ascribed to Sam, "Perry-the-Winkle" (Number eight) and "Cat" (Number twelve — Tolkien insists, however, that "Sam can only have touched up an older piece of the comic bestiary lore of which Hobbits appear to have been fond" [TB, p. 7]) are at about the same level of metrical skill and imagination as Number seven — pleasant and amusing doggerel. Bilbo's Number three, however, is a different matter. Tolkien himself liked the piece so much that he printed it in two different versions, as Number three, "Errantry," in *The Adventures of Tom Bombadil*, and as Bilbo's poem recited at Rivendell in Book II of *The Lord of the Rings*. But the existence of two separate versions of the "ancient" work is more fodder for Tolkien's parodic scholarship, allowing him to continue his theorizing about the "authorship" of the poems in the *Bombadil* volume. Number three, he asserts, was "evidently made by Bilbo. This is indicated by its obvious relationship to the long poem recited by Bilbo, as his own composition, in the house of Elrond. In origin a 'nonsense rhyme', it is in the Rivendell version found transformed and applied, somewhat incongruously, to the High-elvish and Númenorean legends of Eärendil. Probably because Bilbo invented its metrical devices and was proud of them" (TB, p. 8). The humor here turns both inward and outward. First of all, Tolkien continues the device of the assumed reality of elves and Númenor so that he can set up the excellent little joke at the end of this paragraph of his preface, where he comments on the phony elvishness of "Errantry," pointing out with comic editorial pomposity that "Elvish traditions . . . are not seriously treated" in that poem, because the "names used (*Derrilyn, Thellamie, Belmarie, Aerie*) are mere inventions in the Elvish style, and are not in fact Elvish at all." Here the device of assumed separate authorship works deliciously — this is not *my* piece of concocted Elvish nonsense, it is *Bilbo's*, and everybody knows, or else should know, that hobbits are "fond of strange words" (TB, p. 9).

But the joke turns outward, too, toward editors of texts and writers of introductions in general. For the editor of *The Adventures of Tom Bombadil* might very well be "wrong" in his ascription of Number three to Bilbo, and wrong in a way that parodies excessive editorial self-confidence. It is equally possible that the "obvious relationship" between the Rivendell poem and "Errantry" is the other way around, that Bilbo's Rivendell poem is the earlier, and that Number three is a hobbit's vulgarization of the original's Elvish themes and modes. Tolkien the editor of Middle-earth may very well be exposing himself deliberately to the charge of too quick assumptions, and then covering up with a satirically assumed air of scholarly authority: "It was evidently made by Bilbo." But, of course, the joke at this point turns against the reader, for in thinking thus, he is assuming the same sort of stance toward the "reality" of Middle-earth and the "importance" of the doggerel of the Shire that Tolkien so richly parodies in his preface to *Tom Bombadil*. I do not doubt he intended we should be thus trapped by our close reading of his joke.

Whatever the chronological relationship between the poems, their structural and tonal relationship is a fascinating study. "Errantry" is a comic "circle" poem, a "kind which seems to have amused Hobbits: a rhyme or story which returns to its own beginning, and so may be recited until the hearers revolt," as Tolkien describes it in his preface (p. 7). The poem is a comic version of "There and Back Again"; it is, in other words, structurally and tonally like *The Hobbit* (a cyclical quest story, chiefly comic, bearing the subtitle just quoted) and has, perhaps like *The Hobbit*, no other intention than the amusement of its readers. Bilbo's poem about Eärendil, on the other hand (which he recites at Rivendell in I [pp. 246–249]) is a tragic story about an unwanted apotheosis: Eärendil is given, quite without desiring it, a Silmaril; then, after chaotic adventures, he passes to Elvenhome. A ship is built for him, and, all unwillingly, he leaves Middle-earth "to sail the shoreless skies" and "bear his shining lamp afar,/the Flammifer of Westernesse," becoming a star "till Moon should fade." This, of course, sounds much like Frodo's story: Quite without his willing it, Frodo is given the Ring, bears it through chaotic adventures, returns home, and then again, quite without willing or desiring it, must embark upon an elven-ship and pass westward, never to see again the simple haunts of hobbits. In other words, the "stories" of and relationship between "Errantry" and the poem of Eärendil are analogous to the stories of and relationship between *The Hobbit* and *The Lord of the Rings;* the one is a comic account of a "There and Back Again" quest, the other a serious and melancholy account of the unwished-for apotheosis of the bearer of a mighty totem.

But Bilbo's "Errantry" is yet one more thing — a friendly parody of Charles Williams' *Taliessin* poems. Williams was a fellow "Inkling" with Tolkien at Oxford, one of a group of friends that included C. S. Lewis, who met regularly to read their works in progress to each other. Williams' *Taliessin Through Logres* was published in 1938, and a striking feature of its poetry was the trick of rhyming the middle or final word of a line with a middle word in the next line, a trick that Tolkien picked up in "Errantry" and embellished to the point of caricature.

> *Taliessin saw the flash of his style*
> *dash at the wax; he saw the hexameter spring,*
> *and the king's sword swing; he saw, in the long field,*
> *the point where the pirate chaos might suddenly yield,*
> *the place for the law of grace to strike.*
>
> ("Mount Badon")[4]

> *He passed the archipelagoes*
> *Where yellow grows the marigold,*
> *Where countless silver fountains are,*
> *And mountains are of fairy-gold.*
> *He took to war and foraying,*
> *A-harrying beyond the sea,*
> *And roaming over Belmarie*
> *And Thellamie and Fantasie.*
>
> ("Errantry")

This element of friendly parody brings us to Tolkien's next and finest level of humor: several of the poems in the *Bombadil* volume are his own rewritings of some standard and well-known English nursery rhymes and Old English poems, so presented that the reader, suddenly and with a lurch, realizes that he is in the presence of the "real sources" of (and brilliant parody solutions to famous scholarly problems about) the English poems.

The first joke of this sort appears in Number five, "The Man in the Moon stayed up Too Late." In his preface, Tolkien simply informs us that "In the Red Book it is said that No. 5 was made by Bilbo" (p. 7). Here is the quietly subtle and indirect introduction to one of the most elaborate hoaxes in Tolkien's little volume, for a reading of Number five will quickly make one aware that Bilbo in fact "wrote" what appears to be the "original version" of one of our most popular (and hotly debated) nursery rhymes:

> *Hey diddle diddle,*
> *The cat and the fiddle,*
> *The cow jumped over the moon.*
> *The little dog laughed to see such sport,*
> *And the dish ran away with the spoon.*

Iona and Peter Opie have declared that "a considerable amount of nonsense has been written about" this, the "best-known nonsense verse in the language." [5] Tolkien's poem is the *reductio* of all that nonsense, and the point of his joke becomes clear only in the context of the long and involved scholarly debate about the origin and meaning of "Hey Diddle Diddle." For example, as long ago as 1842, James Orchard Halliwell, in his great work *The Nursery Rhymes of England*, theorized that the opening nonsense phrase was a corruption of *Ád' ádela, dêla d'áde*, though the Opies feel that "probably . . . he knew he was being hoaxed when he was presented with a parallel verse in 'ancient' Greek." In addition to Halliwell's attempt, the Opies list no less than six other unlikely, and sometimes absurd, "origin" theories for the rhyme, and three more for the phrase "the cat and the fiddle."[6] Such a farrago is clearly an ideal stage for Tolkien to enter and imply, with tongue firmly in cheek, that with his great discovery of the Red Book marginalia, the problem of the origin and meaning of this poem has forever disappeared. Bilbo Baggins wrote it, and our present worn-down version, nonsense as it stands, will make perfect sense when it is plugged into the proper places of its original, "The Man in the Moon stayed up Too Late." Bilbo's poem supplies a meaningful context, a narrative, into which the meaningless fragment we now have fits perfectly. We learn *why* the cat, cow, dog, dish, and spoon perform their puzzling antics.

Somewhere in Middle-earth, says Bilbo, there is an inn, "a merry old inn/beneath an old grey hill," where

they brew a beer so brown
That the Man in the Moon himself came down
one night to drink his fill.

The beer is so powerful, and has such an effect, that it makes the ostler's "tipsy cat" play a "five-stringed fiddle" and the innkeeper's dog laugh at the drunken jokes of the guests, while the music of the cat's fiddle "turns [the] head" of the innkeeper's cow "like ale," making her "wave her tufted tail/ and dance upon the green." One night, as the setting moon nears the hill above the inn, the Man in the Moon, enticed by that strong beer, steps down for a drink. He has first one, then another, and then rolls "beneath his chair." Drunken, the "Man" will fail to drive the moon behind the hill at its proper setting time before the sun rises, unless he can be wakened:

The ostler said to his tipsy cat:
"The white horses of the Moon,
They neigh and champ their silver bits;
But their master's been and drowned his wits,
and the Sun'll be rising soon!"

So the cat on his fiddle played hey-diddle-diddle,
a jig that would wake the dead:
He squeaked and sawed and quickened the tune,
While the landlord shook the Man in the Moon:
"It's after three!" he said.

The "solution" to the ancient problem of the meaning of "Hey diddle diddle" turns out, in Tolkien's witty *reductio*, to be quite simple after all; the phrase is merely Bilbo's onomatopoeic representation of the fiddle's squawk (echoed in a later stanza as "deedle-dum-deedle"). The other puzzling elements of the rhyme are "solved" just as easily. The wild sawing of the cat's fiddle affects everything at the inn; as the innkeeper rolls the "Man" up the hill and "bundled him into the Moon," the cow follows them, capering "like a deer," and a dish, excited at the music, comes running up with a spoon. The cat saws so vigorously, however, that "With a ping and a pong the fiddle-strings broke!" The cow, startled, "jumped over the Moon," which was sitting atop the hill awaiting the "Man," and the dish, equally startled, "ran off with the silver Sunday spoon." All this amuses the already humorous dog; he "laughed to see such fun." But at last, just in time, "The round Moon rolled behind the hill,/ as the Sun raised up her head." (Tolkien dutifully explains in a footnote to Frodo's version in *The Fellowship* that hobbits, like elves, always refer to the sun as "she.")

Tolkien's joke, however, has not even yet run its course, for it turns out that the bibulous man-in-the-moon device is not original with Bilbo. There is an even more ancient source for our nursery rhymes — Gondor. "The Man in the Moon came down Too Soon," Number six in the Red Book, "must be derived ultimately from Gondor," Tolkien assures us in his preface, for it "actually mentions *Belfalas* (the windy bay of Bel), and the Sea-ward tower, *Tirith Aear*, of Dol Amroth" (p. 8). At this, the joke (and the implicit parody scholarship) mushrooms, for of course Number six is the "original" of our nursery rhyme,

> The man in the moon came down too soon
> And asked the way to Norwich.
> He went by the south and burnt his mouth
> With supping cold plum porridge.

Again, a nonsense verse long debated with nonsense equal to its own finds its true "source" and "explanation" in the Red Book, and Tolkien has made in the process a genuinely satiric comment on literary scholarship, at least scholarship of the sort found in a letter to *Notes & Queries* in 1884, in which the writer pointed out, according to the Opies, that if " 'plum porridge' was the true wording, the rhyme was likely to date from the time before modern cloth had convert- ed plum porridge into plum pudding." [7] Tolkien, with his wonderful discovery of the Red Book marginalia, has forever closed the great plum porridge debate, for the original version of the nursery rhyme provides the final answer to this and all the other problems of sense in our present nonsense poem. Why did the man in the moon want to go to Norwich? Well, clearly because he is a bit of a drunk, and Norwich, as every Englishman knows, is in the middle of a large grain-growing area and is famous for its beer and ale. Why did he come down "too soon"? Why did he go "by the south" to reach a city northeast of London? It all becomes clear in Number six.

In the Gondorean original, the man in the moon, alone in his cold world, covets fire: "crimson and rose and ember-glows . . . flame with burning tongue." But most of all, "He coveted song, and laughter long,/ and viands hot, and wine." Longing for these earthly delights,

> He twinkled his feet, as he thought of the meat,
>   of pepper, and punch galore;
> And he tripped unaware on his slanting stair,
>   and like a meteor,
> A star in flight, ere Yule one night
>   flickering down he fell
> From his laddery path to a foaming bath
>   in the windy Bay of Bel.

The Bay of Bel is in the extreme south of Middle-earth, the wrong way to go in order to get to a northerly city, as the man in the moon learns when he is caught in a fisherman's net. Advised to "get a bed in an inn," he walks all night to the closest town and finds everyone asleep save one greedy cook, who requires "A silver gift the latch to lift,/ a pearl to pass the door." The man in the moon demands "fire and gold and songs of old/ and red wine flowing free," but the greedy cook allows him naught "till he gave both crown and cloak,"

> And all that he got, in an earthen pot
>   broken and black with smoke,
> Was porridge cold and two days old,
>   to eat with a wooden spoon.

The great porridge/pudding debate was merely academic, it seems, the point of the original poem being that the man in the moon got ordinary grain porridge, for since he landed "ere Yule,"

> For puddings of Yule with plums, poor fool,
> he arrived so much too soon.

Tolkien provides the parody solution to another classic scholarly problem with yet another sleight of hand of source creation in Number eleven, "Fastitocalon." This poem, he tells us in his preface, is a "half-remembered fragment" from the Shire, "written carelessly" in a margin of the Red Book (p. 7). This "fragment," however, turns out to be the "real source" of one of the tales in the Greek bestiary called *Physiologus*, which in turn is the source, or so the scholars have believed, of the Old English *Physiologus* in the Exeter Book. Tolkien's great "contribution" is his discovery of the real source of the term "fastitocalon" as the name of the sea-beast whose back is like an island. The meaning of the *supposed* source has been in debate for more than a century now, since one of the triumphs of English philology in the mid-nineteenth century, Christian W. M. Grein's surmise that "fastitocalon" was a corruption of the Greek ἀσπιδοχελώνη.[8] The difficulty with this rare Greek word is that it may mean either "asp turtle" or "shield turtle"; a debate about its meaning raged until well into our own century, culminating perhaps in Albert S. Cook's virtually interminable introduction to the Anglo-Saxon poem "The Whale" in his edition of *The Old English Elene, Phoenix, and Physiologus*, a classic of wildly irrelevant scholarship. The first eleven pages of Cook's preface to "The Whale" section concern not the poem, as one might hope, nor even the sources of the poem, but the possible sources of the sources, and, in one almost unbelievable page, the possible source of the sources of the sources. The next twelve pages (all the rest of what Cook has to say about the poem) present a discussion of whether ἀσπιδοχελώνη should be translated "asp turtle" or "shield turtle." After a long survey of the remarks of such worthies as "Kazwini, an Arab writer of the latter half of the thirteenth century," the curator of the Peabody Museum at Yale (for the length of his fossil shell of *Archelon schyros*), Arngrim Jonas, and Rondelet (who classified sea turtles as medium-sized whales), Cook decides at last that the Greek work must mean "asp turtle."[9] Thus Cook; Old English philology has become a wild-turtle chase. Enter Tolkien, to reduce the debate to absurdity with his great discovery that the Old English "Whale" is not based on the Greek *Physiologus* after all; both, rather, have a common source in an ancient poem of Middle-earth called "Fastitocalon."

It has long been clear that there is some sort of relationship between the classical *Physiologus* and "The Whale" in the Exeter Book; the standard and reasonable assumption has been that the one is the direct source of the other. A Latin version of the *Physiologus* tells us that

> There is a sea-beast in the ocean, called asp-turtle . . . The monster is very large, like an island. Not being aware of this, the seamen fasten their boats to it as to an island, and attach the anchors and their stakes. They build a fire on the back of the sea-monster, in order to boil somewhat for themselves. When he is scorched, he plunges to the bottom, and wrecks the boats.[10]

The Old English poem tells of the "Great Whale," "Fastito-calon":

> *Like a rough rock   is the Whale's appearance,. . .*
> *So it seems to sailors   they see an island,*
> *And they firmly fasten   their high-prowed ships*
> *With anchor-ropes   to the land that is no land,*
> *Hobble their sea-steeds   at ocean's end . . .*
> *There they encamp,   the sea-weary sailors,*
> *Fearing no danger.   They kindle a fire;*
> *High on the island   the hot flames blaze*
> *And joy returns   to travel-worn hearts*
> *Eager for rest.   Then, crafty in evil,*
> *When the Whale feels the sailors   are fully set*
> *And firmly lodged,   enjoying fair weather,*
> *Suddenly with his prey   Ocean's Guest plunges*
> *Down in the salt wave   seeking the depths,*
> *In the hall of death   drowning sailors and ships.*[11]

Tolkien, however, wittily complicates the old problem of the relationship between the two, with his introduction of a *tertium quid*, a poem even older than the classical *Physiologus*, the very title of which "proves" that "Fastitocalon" is not a corruption of ἀσπιδοχελώνη; indeed the reverse seems to be true:

> *Look, there is Fastitocalon!*
> *An island good to land upon,*
> *   Although 'tis rather bare . . .*
>
> *Ah! foolish folk, who land on HIM,*
> *And little fires proceed to trim*
> *   And hope perhaps for tea!*

It may be that His shell is thick,
He seems to sleep; but He is quick,
  And floats now in the sea
    With guile;
And when He hears their tapping feet,
Or faintly feels the sudden heat,
    With smile
    HE dives,
And promptly turning upside-down
He tips them off, and deep they drown,
  And lose their silly lives
    To their surprise.

So Cook's endlessly elaborated scholarship is all for naught. Not Nearchus,[12] but a nameless hobbit of the Shire in the Third Age of Middle-earth, was the first to record the story of the island-turtle; Tolkien has the last laugh at scholarship spun out for its own sake rather than for the elucidation of the poem at hand.[13] And finally, I suppose, he has the ultimate laugh, for the type of scholarship he so richly parodies is suspiciously like the sort required to produce this chapter.

AFTERWORD

THE MANUSCRIPT of this book was completed and given to the publisher just five days before J. R. R. Tolkien's death. One would, ordinarily, after recovering from the immediate shock and sadness of that loss, find this the best time and place for an attempt at an overview of Tolkien and some conclusions. But the last word has not yet been said about this great author, nor can it, until after the publication of his final work, *The Silmarillion*. Hosts of readers have been awaiting this account of the First and Second Ages of Middle-earth since they read of it in Appendix A of *The Return of the King*. But Tolkien did not hurry to finish it; both out of a desire to protect his heirs and an unwillingness to say farewell to Faërie, he delayed publication of his last work until after his passing. We can reflect that one of the best consolations for our loss of his presence will be the appearance of *The Silmarillion*.

Despite the lack of finality, however, we do need a retrospective view of Tolkien's accomplishment, its permanence, and of the literary atmosphere it entered and influenced. It seems clear to me that *The Lord of the Rings* will remain one of the indispensable books for some time to come, but it is not alone of its kind; Tolkien's masterpiece has risen above a sea of subliterature. Unfortunately, most examples of heroic fantasy in our century are rightly the concern of the sociologist not the literary critic. For reasons obvious to anyone with eyes or nose, our age has called forth a flood of escape literature, but most of it caters, in Tolkien's terms, to the deserter not the prisoner. Yet the very impulse to escape is the expression (however unrecognized) of a critical judgment, and there is no real reason why a temporary escape into a well-constructed fantasy world should not enrich and sharpen our critical perceptions, cleanse the windows onto our own world so that we may return refreshed and prepared to engage with what we were allowed to see from a different perspective. Yet though such fantasy, genuinely creative and genuinely cleansing, is conceivable, the times are unpropitious in the extreme. Men everywhere are trying to rewrite the myths — and failing. While demands for temporary and recuperative escape abound, the flood of heroic fantasy elicited by the need (and it is a flood — check the paperback fantasy section of any bookstore) offers us heroes (and prose!) from which literate minds recoil.

Why the need, and why the failure? They are, in fact, twin expressions of a single cultural tragedy. Contemporary self-esteem, the twentieth-century image of man, is probably the lowest and most degraded in history. The work of such myth-breaking giants as Darwin and Freud is now complete (the effects of that work could be neatly graphed against the decline and disappearance of the hero in late nineteenth- and early twentieth-century literature), and we are now well into a period of degrading overcompensation (and pathetic undercompensation) for a real and painful loss. On the subliterary level, we have daydream superheroes (in one form Conan, in another, James Bond), and in serious literature, sad and bumbling schlemiels and antiheroes (Henderson, Yossarian). But the lack of real heroes in an ambience of real literature is a genuine cultural tragedy. Other ages have produced heroic fantasy that is also literature, that tells truth about men and gods and touches the heart without degrading it. There have been heroes whose deeds ennoble the spirit rather than vulgarize it — Beowulf and Sigurd, Odysseus and Amadis — but virtually none in our age. The reasons are not far to seek. A hero is the expression of a culture's ideals about itself, and our ideals about ourselves have all been punctured. Cultural ideals are formulated and understood most efficiently in myths, and we have lost the ability to participate wholeheartedly in mythic belief, lost in fact the key to response to our culture's central mythic system. And that loss, tragic as it is in its own right, opened the door to one that seems to me even greater: a bone-deep cynicism about, a frostbitten insensitivity toward, the capacities of myth for discovery, for transmission of awe, and for molding a worthwhile self.

Most contemporary heroic fantasy is vulgar and debasing not because its bare themes are debasing — struggle against evil, rescue of the good — but because those themes are unsupported by a resonant image of man: they lack a vital superstructure of ideas. Their authors have been unable to penetrate to the core of the mystery of their craft; they have not perceived that it is in fact mythopoeic, that they, the fantasists, are our *Beowulf*-scops, our Snorri Sturlusons. That they are not up to the task is a grotesque understatement. Instead they have done what comes easy, given a knack for narrative. The stories are there, for anyone to use, to vary in his own way; they come a direct route from the unconscious, and the less strong and subtle the censoring, defining intelligence, the more quickly and shallowly one "creates" the tales: the dragon and the maiden, the minotaur in the labyrinth, the ogre in the tower. Every ancient culture has its versions of these and other standard heroic motifs, and many a folk has turned them into great and enduring literature. But in every case, the bare themes climb toward discovery and power on the ancient stairs of myth, of large and ennobling ideas about man and his godlikeness, or his struggle against gods the more unworthy because more strong.

In short, the soil for fantasy in our time is lush but rank, running to dense weeds not strong trees. Fantasy that is worthy of us, that gives us what we need without degrading us, will require of its author not only a strong narrative gift and a vivid imagination but a vision as well, a vision of man's potential nobility, of the kind of heroism suitable to the second half of our century. It seems to me that Tolkien's popularity is an index to his successful pursuit of that vision.

It needs to be said, however, that not all of Tolkien's works give us the kind of greatness we find in *The Lord of the Rings*. His minor writings will continue to be read, but like the minor works of most major figures, only for the light they shed on the great ones. I mean here such things as "Smith" and "Niggle" and *Tom Bombadil*. Tolkien's critical essays have their own importance and would continue to find a small audience even if he had never written any imaginative literature, for they clarify the functions and importance of fantasy in a way that re-emphasizes for us the meaning of such works as *Beowulf*. *The Hobbit* is another matter. Regardless of its status as adult literature, it has already become, and will doubtless remain, a children's classic. My own reaction as an adult reader is dissatisfaction with *The Hobbit*, a feeling that it is little more than a trial run for the *Rings*. Many adult readers, though, do not feel at all unhappy with

The Hobbit and can enter it with intense Secondary Belief. Perhaps no final word is yet possible on this work.

Whether Tolkien is already enjoying the Mountains he envisaged, or is now perfecting his art and his human spirit in the Workhouse, he has earned the lasting gratitude of us all. His name will stand with the great ones.

NOTES

NOTES

Chapter I (pages 1–18)

1. W. P. Ker, *The Dark Ages*, quoted in J. R. R. Tolkien, *"Beowulf*: The Monsters and the Critics," *An Anthology of Beowulf Criticism*, ed. Lewis E. Nicholson (University of Notre Dame Press, 1963), pp. 57–58. Tolkien's lecture first appeared in the *Proceedings of the British Academy*, XXII (1936), 245–95. All references here are to the more readily available reprint and will be identified in the text.
2. Mircea Eliade, *Cosmos and History: The Myth of the Eternal Return* (New York: Harper & Row, 1959), p. 39.
3. J. R. R. Tolkien, *Tree and Leaf* (Boston: Houghton Mifflin, 1965), p. vii. Future references identified in the text by "TL" and page number.
4. In the remarks that follow I am indebted to M. H. Abrams, *The Mirror and the Lamp* (New York: W. W. Norton, 1958). The use of his term "heterocosm" is the first sign of that debt.
5. Quoted in Abrams, p. 273.
6. *The Spectator*, ed. G. Gregory Smith (New York: E. P. Dutton, 1933), III, 84.
7. *The Spectator*, III, 92.
8. Richard Hurd, *Letters on Chivalry and Romance*, ed. Edith J. Morley (London: H. Frowde, 1911), p. 138.

Chapter II (pages 19–40)

1. J. R. R. Tolkien, *The Hobbit* (Boston: Houghton Mifflin, 1966), p. 26. All future references are to this edition and will be identified in the text. All references to *The Lord of the Rings* are likewise from the Houghton Mifflin edition and will be identified in the text by volume and page number.
2. See Chapter III for more on Sauron/Satan.

Chapter III (pages 41–55)

1. Erich Neumann, *The Origins and History of Consciousness* (New York:

Pantheon, 1954), p. 148. Future references to this work will be identified in the text.

2. Northrop Frye, *Anatomy of Criticism* (New York: Atheneum, 1967), p. 194.

3. Joseph Campbell, *The Hero with a Thousand Faces* (New York: Pantheon, 1949), pp. 245–46.

4. See William Empson's chapter "The Child as Swain," in *Some Versions of Pastoral* (New York: New Directions, 1950).

Chapter IV (pages 56–75)

1. Stanley Edgar Hyman, *The Tangled Bank* (New York: Grosset & Dunlap, 1966), p. 427.

2. *Blake; Complete Writings*, ed. Geoffrey Keynes (London: Oxford University Press, 1966), pp. 689, 777.

3. See Harold Bloom, *Yeats* (New York: Oxford University Press, 1970), and Hazard Adams, *Blake and Yeats: The Contrary Vision* (Ithaca: Cornell University Press, 1955), for discussions of Yeats's debt and relationship to Blake.

4. S. Foster Damon, *A Blake Dictionary* (Providence, R.I.: Brown University Press, 1965), p. 309.

5. *The Poetry and Prose of William Blake*, ed. David V. Erdman, commentary by Harold Bloom (New York: Doubleday, 1968), p. 815.

Chapter V (pages 76–108)

1. Eliade, *Cosmos and History: The Myth of the Eternal Return*, pp. 39–40.

2. Frye, *Anatomy of Criticism*, pp. 186–87.

3. Frye, p. 196.

Chapter VI (pages 109–125)

1. *"Beowulf*: The Monsters and the Critics," ed. Lewis E. Nicholson, *An Anthology of Beowulf Criticism* (Notre Dame, Indiana: University of Notre Dame Press, 1963), pp. 52–53.

2. Richard West has said that the story "existed in MS. for many years before JRRT was persuaded to publish it." *Tolkien Criticism: An Annotated Checklist* (Kent, Ohio: Kent State University Press, 1970), p. 7.

3. *Tree and Leaf*, p. vii. All references to "Leaf by Niggle" are from this edition and will be identified in the text by "TL" and page number.

4. J. R. R. Tolkien, *Smith of Wootton Major* (Boston: Houghton Mifflin, 1967), p. 7. All references are to this edition and will be identified in the text.

Chapter VII (pages 126–147)

1. J. R. R. Tolkien, *The Adventures of Tom Bombadil* (Boston: Houghton Mifflin, 1963), p. 7. Future references are to this edition and will be identified in the text by "TB" and page number. Poems quoted from this volume are identified by their number in the text.
2. *"Beowulf*: The Monsters and the Critics," *An Anthology of Beowulf Criticism*, p. 51.
3. William F. Skene, *The Four Ancient Books of Wales* (Edinburgh: Edmonston and Douglas, 1868), I, 3.
4. Charles Williams, *Taliessin through Logres* (London: Oxford University Press, 1938).
5. Iona and Peter Opie, *The Oxford Dictionary of Nursery Rhymes* (London: Oxford University Press, 1952), p. 203.
6. Opie, pp. 203–4.
7. Opie, p. 294.
8. *Sprache*, I, 265, cited in *The Exeter Book*, ed. George Philip Krapp and Elliot Van Kirk Dobbie (New York: Columbia University Press, 1936), p. 316.
9. Albert S. Cook, *The Old English Elene, Phoenix, and Physiologus* (New Haven: Yale University Press, 1919), pp. lxxii–lxxxv.
10. Pitra, *Spicilegium Solesmense*, 3. 352, quoted in Cook, p. lxxiv.
11. Charles W. Kennedy, *An Anthology of Old English Poetry* (New York: Oxford University Press, 1960), p. 99.
12. Cook assures us that there "can be no doubt that the germ of that chapter of the *Physiologus* which is concerned with the sea-monster (or so-called whale) is to be found in a story related by Nearchus, who was admiral of Alexander's fleet" (p. lxiii).
13. One other lovely example of Tolkien's delight in parodying his scholarship and that of his colleagues is to be found in one of his tales I have not discussed, "Farmer Giles of Ham." This comic short story is a sport among Tolkien's imaginative works in that it in no way deals with Middle-earth, being set in Medieval England. It is typical of his humor, though, in its parody of linguistic scholarship. For a full discussion of this aspect of the story, see Paul Kocher, *Master of Middle-Earth* (Boston: Houghton Mifflin, 1972).

INDEX

INDEX

Abrams, M. H., 155
Adams, Hazard, 156
Addison, Joseph, 12
Adventures of Tom Bombadil, The,
    126–47, 151, 157
Alf, 119–20, 124
Alice in Wonderland, 41, 52
allegory, 9, 59, 109–10, 112–25
Amadis, 150
America: A Prophecy, 70–71
Amon Hen, 91
Anatomy of Criticism, 156
Anduin, 34, 90–91, 97, 103–4
Anglo-Saxons, 5; language, 127,
    144–47; literature of, 127, 138,
    144–46; see also Beowulf and Battle
    of Maldon, The
Anthology of Beowulf Criticism, An,
    155, 156
Anthology of Old English Poetry, An,
    157
anti-Faustian myth, 60–61, 63
Aragorn, 8, 81, 81–94 passim, 96, 100,
    102–4
archetypes, 45, 51–52
Arkenstone, the, 25, 36, 38–40, 44,
    47, 53–54
Arnold, Matthew, 15
áspidochelóne, see "Fastitocalon"
asymmetrical plot, 54
authorial intrusion, 26–28, 30–32, 35

Bag End, 23, 25–26; as womb sym-
    bol, 41–43

Baggins, see Bilbo; Frodo
Balaclava, 65
Balrog, 22
Ban of the Valar, 68
Bard, 39
Barrow-downs, 88
Barrow-wight, 21, 88, 91, 131
Battle of Britain, 62
Battle of Five Armies, The, 22, 35
Battle of Maldon, The, 61, 63, 65–66
Belfalas, 142–43
Beorhtnoth, 65–66
Beorhtwold, 65
Beorn, 22
Beowulf, ix, x, xi, 2–7, 15, 49–50,
    61–66, 109, 114, 150–51
Beowulf poet, the, 2, 5
"Beowulf: The Monsters and the
    Critics," 2–7, 9–10, 109, 155, 156,
    157
Bilbo, xi, 1, 21–29 passim, 80, 82, 98,
    111, 119–20, 124, 126; growth
    toward heroism, 33–40, 53–54; as
    poet, 129, 133–42
Biographia Literaria, 77
birth, 42–45
Black Book of Carmarthen, 127
Black Gate, 107
Blackmur, R. P., 56, 58–59, 61, 66,
    68–69, 72, 75
Black Riders, 84, 86, 89–90
Blake, William, 12, 15–16, 18, 57–
    59, 74–75, 156; Blake's Orc, 69–
    72, 75

Blake and Yeats: The Contrary Vision,
　156
Bloom, Harold, 69, 156
Bombadil, Tom, 22, 55, 86–88, 130–
　32, 134–35
"Bombadil goes Boating," 129, 135
Boromir, 66, 90–93
Bosworth, Joseph, 127
Brandywine, 130
Bree, 8, 88, 110–11, 116–17
Breredon ("Briar Hill"), 130
British Academy, 2, 5, 7, 61, 63, 114
Buckland, 130–32
burglar (Bilbo as), 25, 44, 50
Butterbur, Barliman, 88
Bywater, 42

Campbell, Joseph, 51–52, 156
Caradhras, 90
"Cat," 129, 135
Cater, Bill, x
cave, as symbol, 34, 44
Cave Troll, 55, 91
Chambers of Fire, 108
Cheynes, T. K., 56
"Child as Swain, The," 156
Christianity, 6, 15–18, 58, 67, 112,
　115, 118
Churchill, Winston, 62
Cirith Ungol, 99, 106–7
Cockayne, Oswald, 127
Cockney dialect, 27
"cold counsel," 102, 105
Coleridge, Samuel Taylor, 11, 77
comedy, 26–28, 30–32, 36, 105, 128–
　32, 137–44
Cook, Albert S., 144–47, 157
*Cosmos and History: The Myth of the
　Eternal Return,* 155, 156
Council of Elrond, 83, 86, 100
Crack of Doom, 100, 108

Damon, S. Foster, 69, 156
Dante, 11
Darwin, Charles, 56–57, 149

Dawson, Christopher, 16–17
Dead Marshes, 97–98
Déagol, 34
Deephollow, 130
Delectable Mountains, 117
demons, 12
Denethor, 100–101
Denmark, 3
Dernhelm, *see* Éowyn
Dingle, the, 130
Dol Amroth, 142
Dori, 47
dragons, 1, 3–7, 50–53, 61, 63–64,
　114; *see also* Smaug
Drayton, Michael, 132
Dryden, John, 12
Dúnedain, 104
Dunharrow, 102–3
dwarves, 10, 23, 27, 42–44 *passim,*
　47, 50

Eärendil, 135, 137
Eddas, The, ix
Eliade, Mircea, 5, 81, 155, 156
Eliot, George, 129
Elrond, 21, 28, 47, 82–84 *passim,*
　86–87, 90, 92, 100, 103, 133, 135
Elvenhome, 137
Elvenking, 38, 44
elves, 10, 15, 23, 84–85, 87, 135–36;
　elvish songs, 29–31
Empson, William, 41, 52, 156
Emyn Muil, 97–98
Encyclopedia Biblica, 56
Entdraught, 95, 105–6
Ents, 15, 92, 95
Éomer, 92–93, 96
Éowyn, 101–2
Eros, 74
"Errantry," 130, 132, 135–38
escape literature, 16–17, 30, 149
eucatastrophe, 17–18
evil, 7, 17, 28, 32–33, 35, 74, 87,
　92–94, 97–99; radical evil, 3–4,
　61–62, 66–67
Exeter Book, The, 144–45, 157

Faërie, x, 8–10, 14–18, 30, 53, 110–11, 118–24, 148
Fáfnisbani, 5
fairies, 10, 12, 76
fairy-stories, 14–18, 24, 28, 46, 53
Fangorn, 15, 92–94, 99
fantasy, 2, 9–10, 12–18 *passim*, 20, 30, 110, 117–18, 128; structure of, 76–81, 89, 148–52
Faramir, 99–101
"Farmer Giles of Ham," 157
Farmer Maggot, 130
"Fastitocalon," 129, 144–47
fays, 10
Feast of Good Children, The, 120
Fellowship of the Ring, The, 54, 127–28, 141; *see also Lord of the Rings, The*
Ferny, Bill, 89
Fire-drake, *see* dragons
Flammifer of Westernesse, 137
folk-lore, 7, 24; *see also* fairy-stories
Ford of Bruinen, 89–91
Four Ancient Books of Wales, The, 127, 157
Frazer, Sir James George, 56
Freud, Sigmund, 45, 56–57, 68, 70, 74, 149
Frodo, 8, 21–23, 26–28 *passim*, 30, 34–35, 38, 45, 54–55, 80, 82–93 *passim*, 96–98, 100, 104–8, 111, 116, 119, 124, 126, 134, 141; as anti-Faustian hero, 59–61, 63, 65–66, 71–73
Frye, Northrop, 83, 87, 156

Gamgee, Samwise, *see* Sam
Gandalf, 8, 22–23, 25–28 *passim*, 34–35, 39, 43–44, 47, 80–83, 87, 89–96 *passim*, 100–102, 104–5, 107, 120, 124, 132
Gautland, 3
Geats, 64
Gildor, 85
Gimli, 93, 96
Glóin, 25
Glorfindel, 89

goblins, 31–32, 47
God, 6, 120–21; as poet, 11–12
Gods, 76
Goldberry, 131
Gollancz, Israel, Memorial Lecture, *see* "*Beowulf*: The Monsters and the Critics"
Gollum, 21–23, 25, 32–35, 44, 49, 53, 80, 82, 97–99, 108
Golux, 87
Gondolin, 32
Gondor, 90, 92, 96, 100–105, 142–43
Gorgoroth, 96, 100, 104, 106–7
Gospels, 18
Great Cake, the, 120
Great Goblin, the, 38, 46
Green Dragon, The, 129
Grein, Christian W. M., 144
Grendel, 3, 61, 63
Grishnákh, 94
Gundwall, 130

Hades, 84
halflings, *see* hobbits
Halliwell, James O., 139
Haradrim, 103–4
Helm's Deep, 92–93, 96
Heraclitus, 84
hero, 4–5, 22–23, 48, 50–53, 61, 81, 149–50
Hero with a Thousand Faces, The, 156
"Hey Diddle Diddle," 139–43
Hobbit, The, 155; development of, 1–4, 6–8, 61–62, 64, 66, 121–23, 151–52; as prototype for *Lord of the Rings*, 19–40, 80, 114, 137; psychoanalytic criticism of, 41–55
Hobbiton, 23, 46, 73–74, 83, 85, 89, 120, 133
hobbits, 8, 21, 38–39, 42, 101, 133; poetry of, 130–47
holiday, Bilbo's and the Master Cook's, 119–20, 124
Huorns, 96
Hurd, Richard, 13, 76, 155
Hyman, Stanley Edgar, 56–57, 156

id, 68–70
identity, 42–43
imagination, x, 1–18 *passim*, 23, 32–
33, 35–36, 39, 57–59, 67–69, 79–
81, 110–11, 117–18, 124, 135; *see
also* mythological imagination
Imrahil, Prince, 105
Industrial Revolution, 73–74
intent, law of, 79–80
internal laws, 79–83, 92–93, 95–98,
101–3, 106–8
invisibility, 53, 81, 87
Isengard, 92–94
Isenmouthe, 107
Ithilien, 99
Ivy Bush, The, 129, 133

Jerusalem, William Blake's, 74
Jonas, Arngrim, 145
Jung, Carl, 45

Kazwini, 145
Kennedy, Charles W., 157
Ker, W. P., 3, 65, 155
key, as symbol, 44, 46, 50
Kocher, Paul H., 157

Lake-Town, 38
Landino, Cristoforo, 11–12
Lang, Andrew, Lecture, *see* "On
Fairy-Stories"
language, 9, 14, 20
languages of Middle-earth, 130;
Dark Tongue, 30, Elven-tongue,
31, 133, 135–36, 141; Gondolin,
32, Hobbit, 32, 141
Laocoön, The, 12, 15
Last Homely House, 21
Lawrence, D. H., 73–74
leaf, as symbol, 19, 23, 33, 111,
113–14, 122–23
"Leaf by Niggle," 19, 110–19, 122,
125, 151–52
Lebennin, 103
Legolas, 93, 104
lembas, 100

Letters on Chivalry and Romance, 13,
76, 155
Lewis, Clive Staples, 16, 56, 138
libidinal energy, 70–71
literary criticism, 62, 109; psychoanalytic criticism, 41–55
Lonely Mountain, 50
"Long-Expected Party," the, 21
Lord of the Rings, The, ix, xi, 1–2,
119–24, 129, 137, 157; development of, 6–8, 10, 14–16, 20–40,
110–14, 116–17; anti-Faustian
myth in, 56, 58–63, 65–66, 71–73;
structure of, 76, 79–108, 148–49,
151
Luvah, 70

Malpasso, dragon of, 5
"Man in the Moon came down Too
Soon, The," 142
"Man in the Moon stayed up Too
Late, The," 139–42
Marriage of Heaven and Hell, The, 74
Marx, Karl, 56
Master Cook, 119–20, 124
Master of Middle-Earth, 157
maturation, 37, 53–54; symbols of,
42–55; rites of, 45–46, 55
Meduseld, 96
Meriadoc, *see* Merry
Merry, 86, 88, 90, 92–97, 99–103,
105–6
middangeard, ix
Middle-earth, ix, x, 2, 6, 22, 24, 26,
32, 37–38, 58, 62–63, 87, 117,
122–123, 128–30, 136, 143, 147;
history of, 15, 33–35, 68, 71, 148;
internal laws of, 79–83, 92–93,
95–98, 101–3, 106–8; *see also* Faërie
Middle-earth in *Beowulf,* ix
Milton, John, 32–33, 67–68
Mirkwood, 15, 21–22, 44
Mirror and the Lamp, The, 155
Misty Mountains, 21, 31, 34, 44, 47,
55

Mithe, 130

monsters, 3–7 *passim*

moral, morality, 25, 27, 33, 35, 38, 55, 59, 92, 121; moral law, 79–81

Morannon, 23, 98–100, 104, 107

Mordor, 65, 71–72, 93, 97–100 *passim,* 104–8 *passim*

Morgul, 89

Moria, 22, 91, 97

Mount Doom, 23, 55, 71, 83, 105–8

Müller, Max, 9

myth, x, xi, 2–18, 37, 66–67, 74; and religion, 11–18; psychoanalytic interpretation of, 45–46, 50–52, 55; "broken" myths, 56–58, 149–51

mythological imagination, 2–18, 51–53, 58, 67–69, 81

nature, 13, 59–60, 73–74, 76, 87, 90

Nazgûl, 81, 102

Nearchus, 147, 157

Necromancer, *see* Sauron

Neumann, Erich, 45–46, 53, 156

Niggle, 111–19, 125

Nine Walkers, the, 89–93

Nokes, 120

Norwich, 142–43

"Note on the Shire Records," 127–28

Númenoreans, 68, 135–36

Nursery Rhymes of England, The, 139

oathbreakers, 103–4

Odysseus, 150

Oedipus complex, 45ff.

Old Bullroarer, 95

Old English Elene, Phoenix, and Physiologus, The, 144–47, 157

Old Forest, 22, 55, 86, 90–91

Old Man Willow, 22, 55, 86, 88, 90–91, 131

Old Norse, 119

"Oliphaunt," 129

One, the, 80

One Ring, the, *see* Ring, the

"On Fairy-Stories," xi, 1, 2, 8–18, 19, 30, 77, 110, 117–18, 121–23, 132

"On the Pleasures of the Imagination," 12

Opie, Iona and Peter, 139–40, 157

Orcrist, 47

orcs, 15, 21, 94–97 *passim,* 106–7; as id projection, 68–72; Blake's Orc, 69–72

Original Sin, 68

Origins and History of Consciousness, The, 45ff., 156

Orodruin, 65, 92, 102, 106–7; *see also* Mount Doom

Owl and the Nightingale, The, 113

Oxford Dictionary of the Christian Church, 56

Oxford Dictionary of Nursery Rhymes, The, 157

Oxford English Dictionary, 69

Oxford University, 73, 138

palantír, 93, 96, 100, 103–4

Paradise Lost, 67

Parish, 112–17

parody, Tolkien's, 126–47, 157

Parth Galen, 90, 92–93

Paths of the Dead, 103

Peabody Museum, 145

Pegasus, 16

Pelennor Fields, 93, 102–3

Perilous Realm, *see* Faërie

"Perry-the-Winkle," 135

"Peter Rabbit," 49

phallic symbols and symbolism, 43–44, 48–49, 55

phial of Galadriel, 107

Physiologus, 144–46

Pilgrim's Progress, 117

Pippin, 86, 88, 90, 92–97, 99–103, 105–6

Pitra, 157

pity, exhibited by Bilbo, 35, 80;

pity (contd.)
exhibited by Aragorn, 93; exhibited by Frodo, 98
Prancing Pony, The, 88, 90
Precious, the, 34, 99, 108; *see also* Ring, the
pride, exhibited by Beowulf, 64–65; of trees in Old Forest, 87
"Princess Mee," 132–33
proverbs, used in Secondary World, 79, 81, 92–94, 96, 98, 101–3, 107–8
Providence, 79–80, 82–83, 86, 92, 94–95
purgatory, *see* Workhouse

quest, pattern in *Hobbit* and *Rings*, 21–22, 37; aided by Bombadil, 86, 88; pattern in Books I and II of *Rings*, 90–93; furthered by Frodo's pity and mercy, 98–99; Sam's companionship on, 134

Rawlinson Chair, 1, 127
realism, 76–78
Red Book of Hergest, 127
Red Book of Westmarch, 126–28, 132, 134, 139–40, 142, 144
religion, 5; and mythology, 13–15; and fantasy, 17–18; and modern man, 56–58
renunciation, in *The Hobbit*, 37–40; in *The Lord of the Rings*, 54
repression, 70, 72
Return of the King, The, 148; *see also Lord of the Rings, The*
riddle game, 21–22
Ring, the, 1, 8, 21–26 *passim*, 32–35, 38, 44, 47–48, 53–54, 59–60, 80, 82–84, 87–93 *passim*, 104–6, 108, 119, 124, 137; history of, 34–35
Ringbearer, 83, 85, 87–92 *passim*, 98–99, 105, 108; *see also* Bilbo; Frodo; Gollum
rites of initiation, 45–46, 55

Rivendell, 21, 23, 27–28, 30, 47, 83, 89, 119–20, 135–37
Rohan, 92, 97, 100–103
Rohirrim, 94–96, 102

Sackville-Bagginses, 25, 44
Sam, 63, 65–66, 71, 84–86, 88, 90–93, 96–100, 104–7; as poet, 129, 133–35
Sammath Naur, 108; *see also* Chambers of Fire
Saruman, 72–73, 92–93, 95–98 *passim*, 99
Satan, 66–68; in Milton, 32–33, 67–68
Sauron, 7, 21–22, 30, 60, 63, 71, 84, 86–87, 90–92, 107–8; as satanic figure, 32–34, 66–68, 155
Sea of Windless Storm, the, 123
Secondary Belief, 11, 78, 152; *see also* Secondary World
Secondary World, 11, 13, 20, 32, 118–19, 122; structure of, 77–81, 89
Shakespeare, William, 132
Shelob, 86, 98–99
Shire, 21, 25–26, 60, 69, 73–74, 84–85, 87, 101, 105–6, 128–29, 132–34, 144, 147
Shirebourn, 130
Sigurd, 150
Silmaril, 137
Silmarillion, The, 118, 149
Sir Gawain and the Green Knight, 127
Skene, William, 127, 157
Smaug, 21–22 *passim*, 25, 38, 44, 46, 49–50 *passim*, 53
Sméagol, *see* Gollum
Smith of Wootton Major, 110, 118–25, 151, 157
Snorri Sturluson, 150
Some Versions of Pastoral, 156
Spectator, The, 12, 155
spell, as defined by Tolkien, 14; of Faërie, 110

Spenser, Edmund, 76
Spicilegium Solesmense, 157
spiders, 21, 25, 44; *see also* Mirkwood
Sting, 98
"Stone Troll, The," 134–35
Strider, *see* Aragorn
subcreation, 11, 13; *see also* Secondary World
sword, as symbol, 43–44, 48–49, 55;
Sting, 98; of Westernesse, 102
symbols, of evil, 33–34, 59; psychoanalytic, 41–52; mythic, 51–55;
Christian, 58, 115–18

Taliessin Through Logres, 138, 157
Tangled Bank, The, 56–57, 156
Thanatos, 74
Théoden, 23, 81, 92, 95–96, 100–103
Thorin, 23, 25, 36–39, 50
Thror's Map, 50
thumb-sucking, 42
Thurber, James, 87
Tirith Aear, 142
Tolkien, J. R. R.: imagination of, x,
1–18, 23, 32, 33, 35–36, 51–53,
57–59, 67–69, 79–81, 110–11,
117–18, 124, 135; religion of, 5–6,
12–18, 67, 112, 118; poetry of,
29–30, 126–47; accomplishment
of, 148–52
*Tolkien Criticism: An Annotated
Checklist*, 156
tone, in *The Hobbit*, 26–29, 35–36
Took, 25, 35
totem, 45ff., 49, 138
treasure, as symbol, 46, 49, 53

Tree and Leaf, 8, 14–18, 20, 24, 110,
155, 156; *see also* "On Fairy-
Stories"
Treebeard, 15, 92, 94–95, 99; *see also*
Fangorn
trolls, 10, 27, 43–44, 49; *see also* Cave
Troll; "Stone Troll, The"

Undying Lands, 68
"Unexpected Party," the, 21
University of Saint Andrews, 8
Urthona, 70
Uruk-hai, 72, 93
Uttermost West, 23

Valar, 80; *see also* Ban of the Valar
Vaughans, 127
Völsunga Saga, The, ix

Watcher, the, 91
Weathertop, 89, 91
West, Richard, 156
"Whale, The," 144–46
Wiglaf, 65
Williams, Charles, 138, 157
witches, 10, 12, 76
Withywindle, 55, 130–31
womb symbols, 41–48
Wootton Major, 119–20; *see also*
Smith of Wootton Major
Workhouse, 115–17, 152
worms, *see* dragons
Wormtongue, 96
wraiths, 84, 89, 98; *see also* Nazgûl

Yeats, William Butler, 58, 156

DATE		
FEB 1 '88		
MAR 1 '88		
AUG 15 '94		
NOV 20		
NOV 20		
NOV 21		
JUL 0		
APR 1 1 2001		

49013